KALEIDOSCOPIC DESIGNS
AND HOW TO CREATE THEM

Illustrations by
Norma Yvette Finkel

Text by
Leslie G. Finkel

Dover Publications, Inc.
New York

Published in Canada by General Publishing Company, Ltd., 30 Lesmill Road, Don Mills, Toronto, Ontario.
Published in the United Kingdom by Constable and Company, Ltd.

Kaleidoscopic Designs and How to Create Them is a new work, first published by Dover Publications, Inc., in 1980.

DOVER *Pictorial Archive* SERIES

International Standard Book Number: 0-486-23935-7

Manufactured in the United States of America
Dover Publications, Inc.,
31 East 2nd Street,
Mineola, N.Y. 11501

HOW TO CREATE KALEIDOSCOPIC DESIGNS

The kaleidoscope as we know it today was patented by Sir David Brewster in 1817. This still-popular toy is a cylinder containing two mirrors that meet at an angle and run the length of the tube. There is an eyehole at one end and small bits of colored glass between two flat pieces of glass at the other. As the kaleidoscope is rotated, the colored glass falls in different patterns that are reflected in the mirrors. When viewing through the eyehole and against a light source, one sees a constantly changing series of circular designs composed of four, six, eight or more wedge-shaped sections, the number depending on the angle at which the mirrors have been placed.

This book tells you how to create circular kaleidoscopic designs on paper, step by step. Although the finished art looks excitingly intricate, the technique is simple and easily mastered. Best of all, it doesn't involve any freehand drawing at all, so even persons with no drawing ability will find that they can quickly create handsome designs suitable for framing!

LIST OF MATERIALS

Your local dime store or art supply shop should have all these inexpensive items in stock.

- white poster board
- tracing paper
- carbon paper
- scissors
- #2 (soft or medium-soft) graphite or black lead pencils
- eraser
- ballpoint pen
- black fine point marker (such as Pilot razor-edge pen)
- ruler
- compass
- protractor
- X-Acto knife
- 2 small rectangular mirrors
- masking tape

CHOOSING A "PICTURE WEDGE"

The circular designs are created by *tracing* wedge-shaped sections from illustrations you find in books, newspapers, magazines, greeting cards, etc. Source illustrations can be in black and white or in color, but if they are in color (or have a lot of shading) trace only the outlines of the shapes themselves, and ignore the tonal areas.

To help you get started right away, this book contains three different sized wedges at the back of this book. First cut on the dashed lines, and then cut out the wedge shapes, thus creating "windows" through which you can view sections of possible source illustrations.

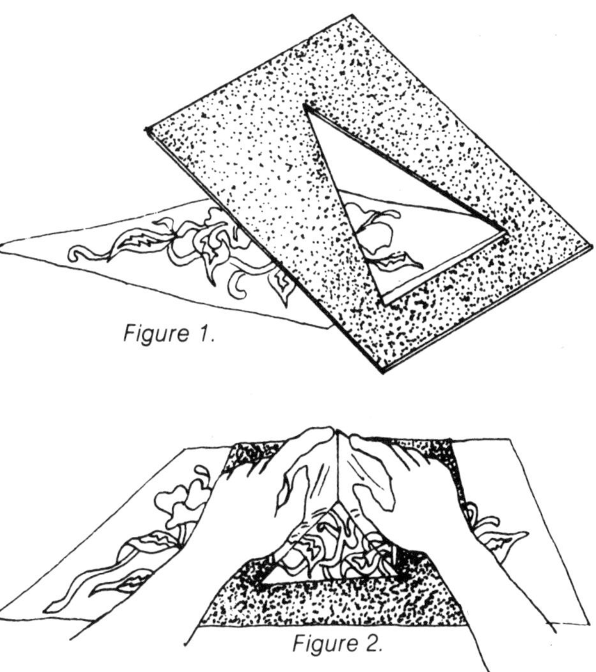

Figure 1.

Figure 2.

Any section of any design will automatically create a kaleidoscopic effect when repeated in circular fashion, but the most striking designs are made from rather intricate source illustrations, whereas the least interesting designs are those based on very simple source pictures with large blank areas.

Select a picture segment by laying "windows" over areas of different possible source illustrations until you find a wedge that appeals to you (Figure 1). Make sure that the pattern fills the wedge, because small designs "floating" in empty space don't make very interesting kaleidoscopic designs. Next, "preview" what the finished circular design will look like by positioning small rectangular mirrors along the two straight sides of the wedge, as in Figure 2.

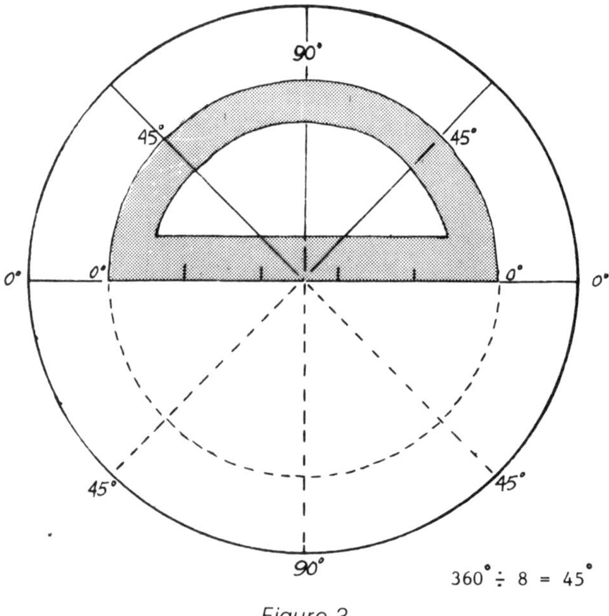

Figure 3.

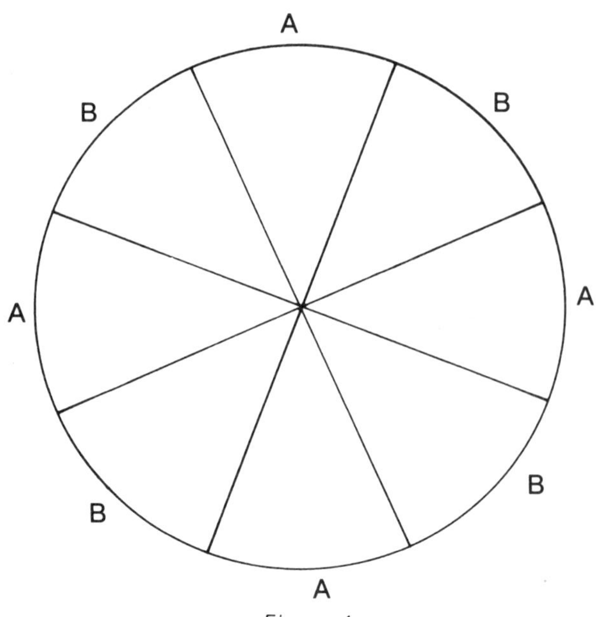

Figure 4.

Once you've firmly decided on a picture wedge, note whether you're using window #1, #2, or #3. Window #1 will make up into a four-part circle measuring 6″ across, whereas #2 will give a six-part design measuring 9″. Window #3 works up into a 12-inch design with eight parts or segments. Tape the "window" in position over the picture with a couple of pieces of masking tape.

Now take a square piece of poster board about two or three inches larger than the circle—say a 15″-square board for an eight-wedge (12″) design. Using a ruler, draw a straight pencil line across the middle of the square on the *dull* side of the board. (The dull side is best because it takes color and ink well without running.) Measure the line and mark the center point. Next, with your compass set to half the desired diameter (6″ for a 12″ circle), draw a circle in pencil, making sure that the point of the compass is on the center point of the pencil line. Keep all pencil lines as light as possible; they will have to be erased later on.

Now you need to divide the circle into the desired number of wedge-shaped sections. Use a protractor to do this. Center it on the straight pencil line and, for eight wedges, put a pencil mark at both 45° marks and one at the 90° mark (Figure 3). (For a six-wedge design, mark both 60° points, and use only the 90° point for a four-wedge design.) Next, invert the protractor and do the same thing again in the bottom half of the circle. Now connect opposite pencil marks with straight pencil lines running across the circle. Do this entire procedure carefully and neatly, and check your work to make sure it is accurate. Label alternate segments A and B, as in Figure 4.

Next, take a piece of tracing paper and carefully trace any one of the wedges from the circle: then, using carbon paper, transfer the wedge shape onto a small piece of poster board. With a sharp X-Acto knife, neatly cut the wedge shape out of the poster board. (Make sure there is a scrap piece of cardboard underneath the blade so you don't mar the table surface.)

The wedge which you've just cut from the poster board will be just like the "window" you used to select your picture segment, but because it's on heavier paper it will be more convenient to use from this point on. For future use on other designs, label it now according to number of wedges and diameter of circle.

The next step is to trace the picture segment you've selected. After mentally recording its position, remove the first "window" and place a piece of tracing paper over the picture area; then put the poster board "window" in place on top of the tracing paper. Secure everything with tape at the edges. Using a #2 (soft) pencil, trace both the design itself and the wedge shape. Keep your drawing "flat" and linear by tracing only the outlines in the pattern and ignoring lines that are meant to indicate shading and give depth. Trace around rather than fill in any solid black areas, as you may decide to color these parts differently later on. Then remove the tracing paper, turn it over and retrace it onto another sheet of paper. Mark the first tracing "A" and the second, its mirror image, "B" (see Figure 5). The kaleidoscopic design will be created by alternating traced copies of "A" and "B" around a circle.

ASSEMBLING THE CIRCULAR DESIGN

Take the traced segment labeled A and fit it into any one of the circle segments labeled A. Make sure the two wedge shapes fit each other perfectly all around, then attach the tracing to the poster board with a couple of small strips of masking tape along one side. Next, slip a piece of carbon paper (carbon side down) underneath the tracing paper, and trace over the tracing paper design with a ballpoint pen. *Don't* retrace the outline of the wedge shape.

After tracing the design as neatly and as accurately as you can, carefully remove the carbon paper *without untaping the tracing.* Check to see if the whole design has been legibly transferred to the poster board. Replace the

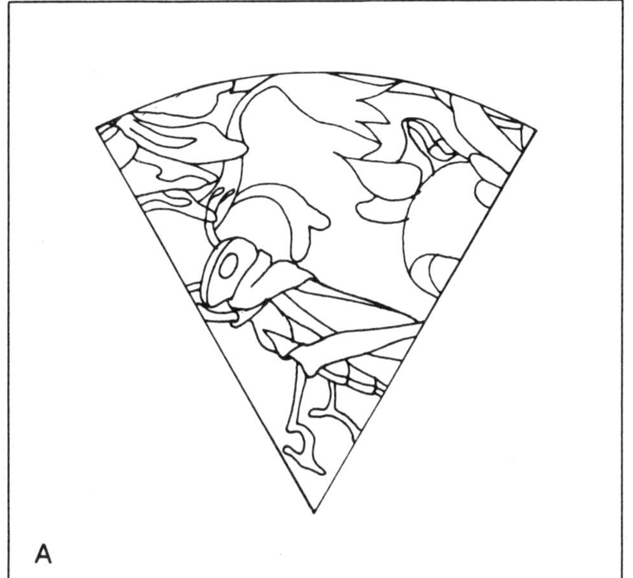

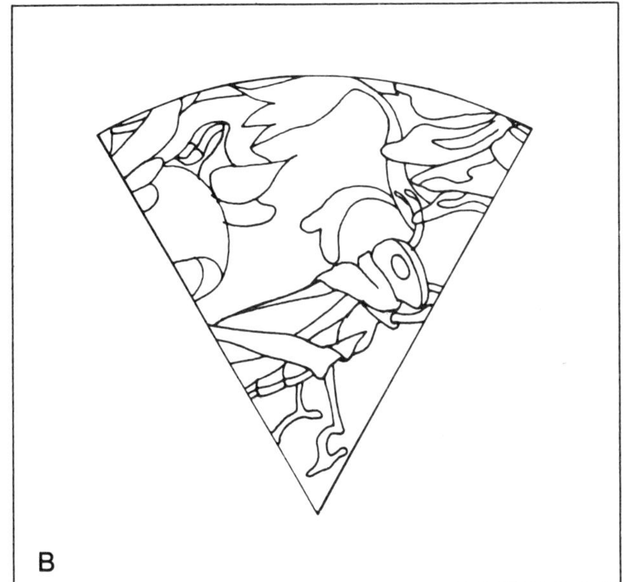

Figure 5.

carbon and carefully retrace over any areas that are weak or incomplete.

Next, remove the tracing and carbon papers and carefully go over the entire carboned design with a black fine point marker such as the Pilot razor-edge pen. This will keep the carboned image from smearing and will render it permanent. Work neatly and accurately.

Now repeat the procedure, using tracing B in an adjacent wedge. Work around the circle either clockwise or counterclockwise, wedge by wedge. Don't try to trace all the like-numbered wedges at once and then fill in with the others, as distortion will occur and mar the final design. Remember to go over each carboned wedge design with the fine point marker immediately after it's completed to keep it from smearing.

After all the wedges have been filled and inked in, carefully erase all pencil lines. If you've copied the design carefully on tracing paper and transferred it neatly and accurately, everything should fit together perfectly, but you may find it necessary to touch up lines here and there to make them blend or join smoothly.

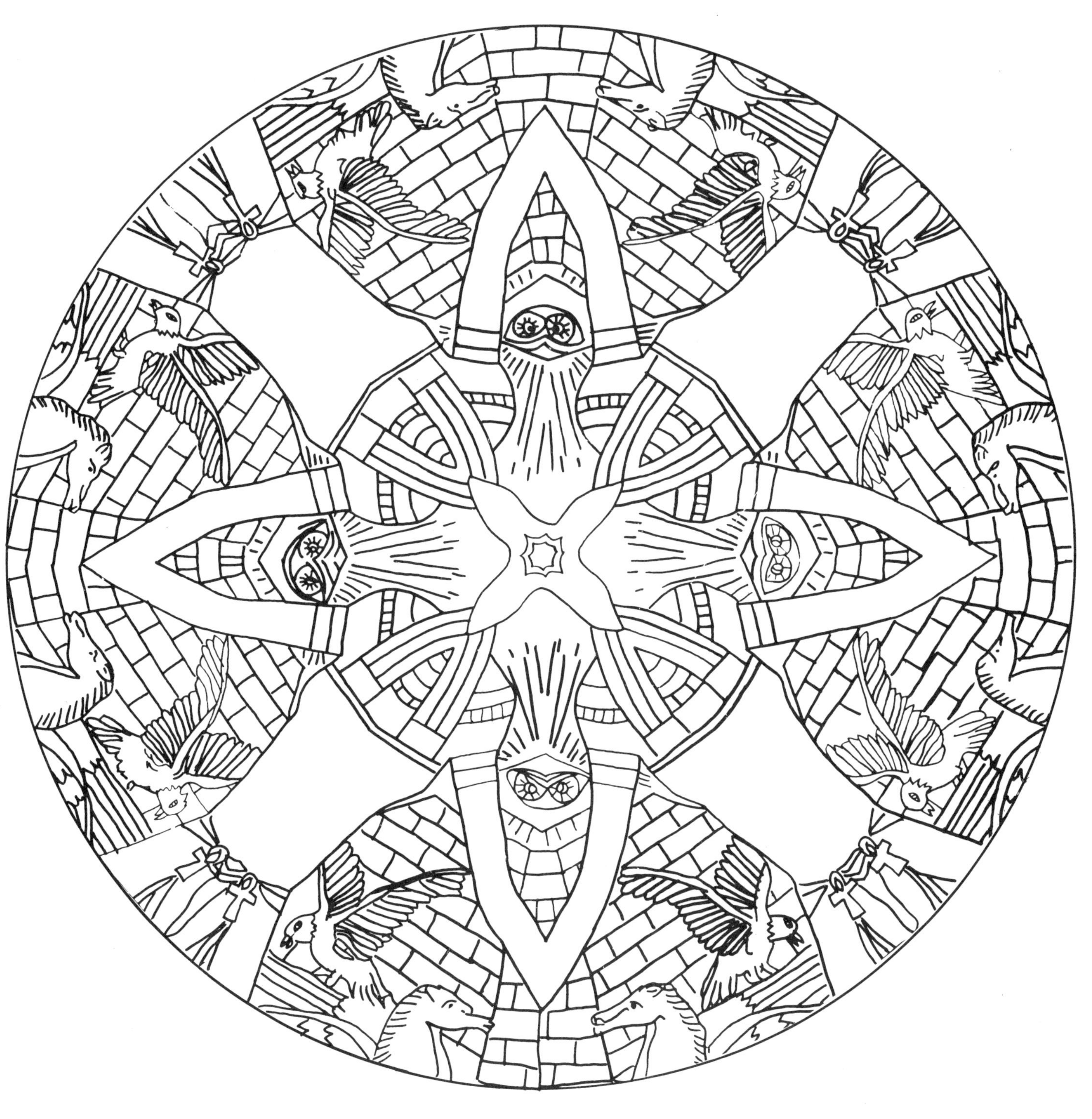

PLATE 1 ''Tutankhamen.''

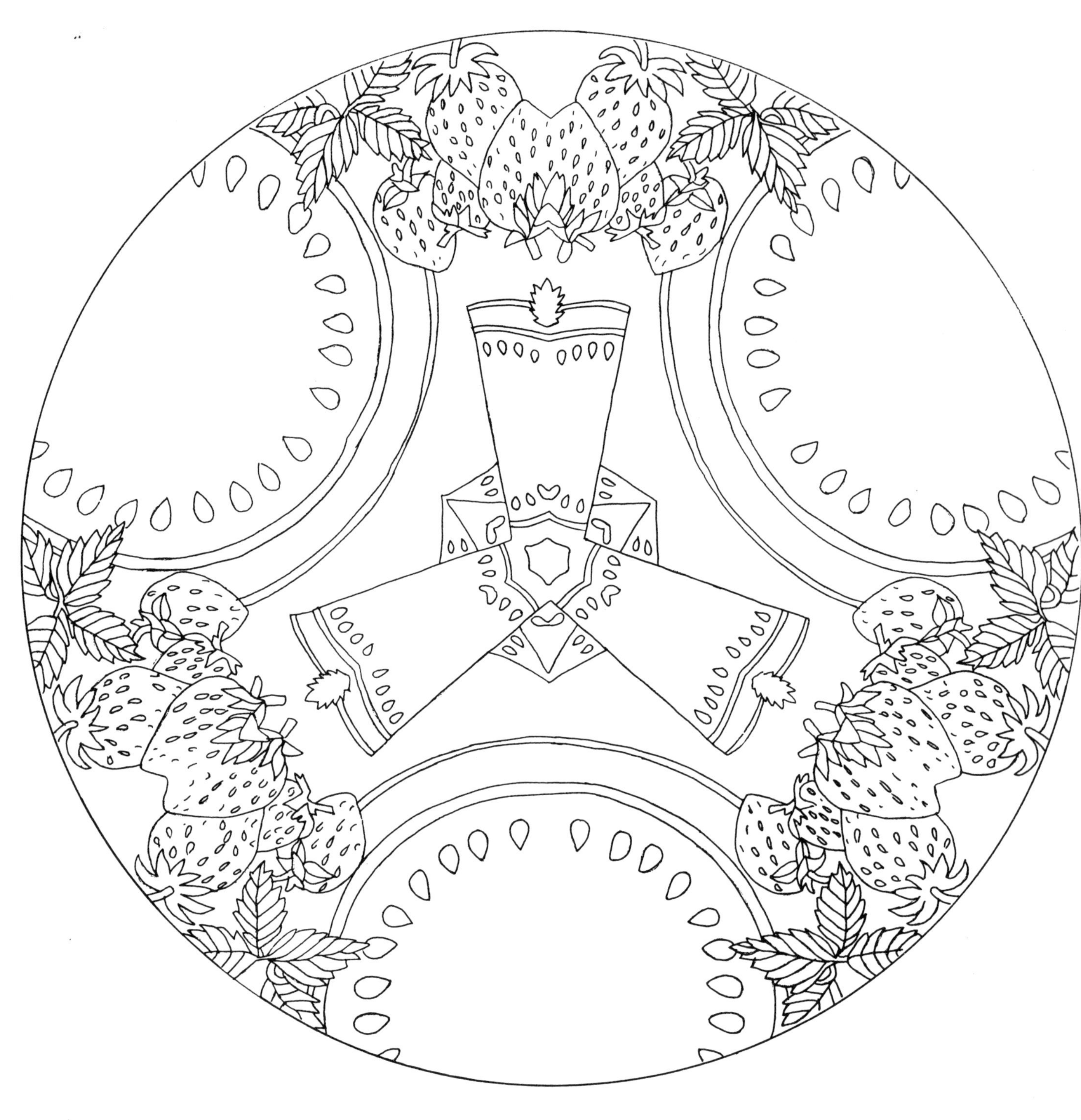

PLATE 2 ''Melons and Berries.''

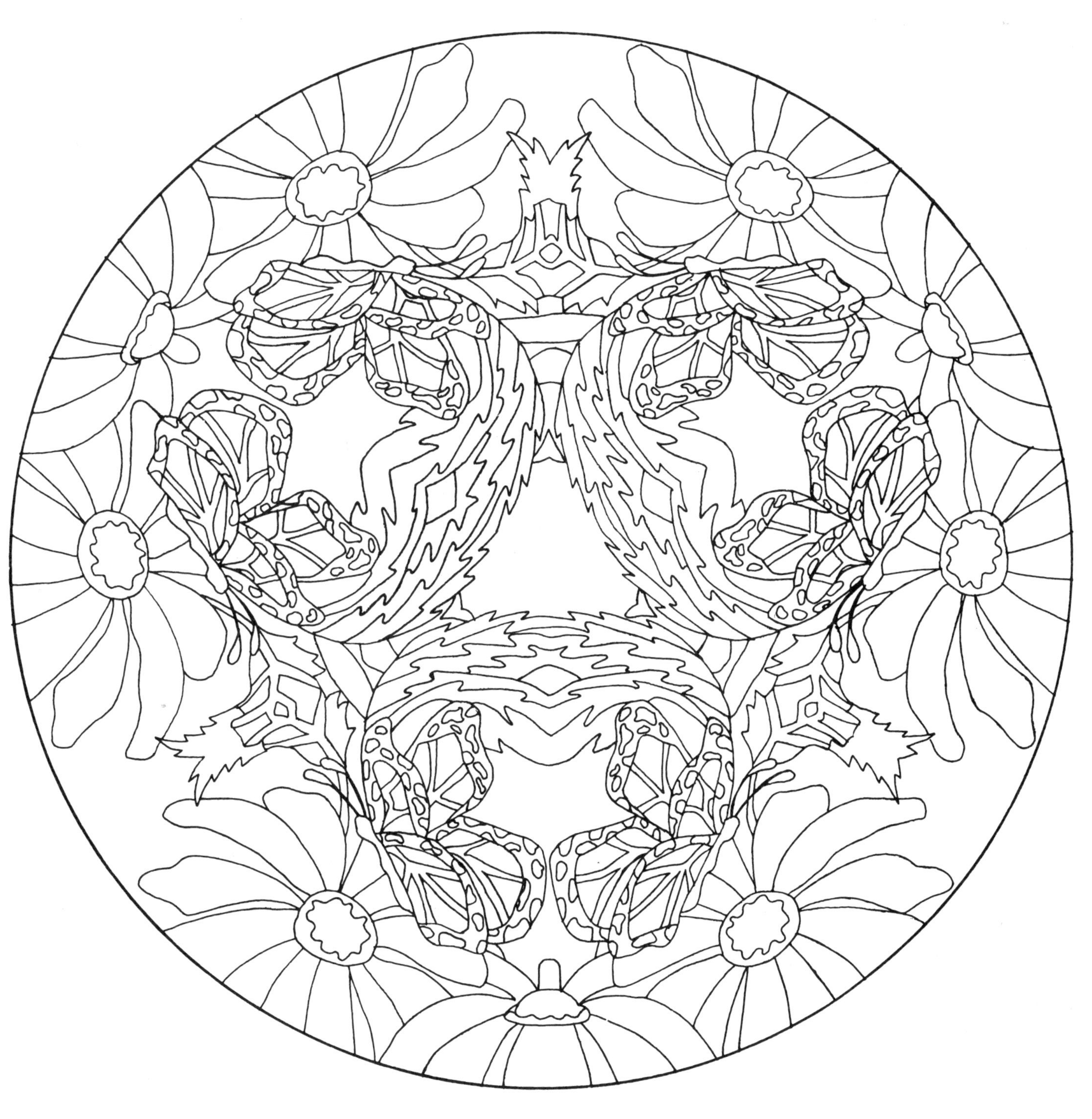

PLATE 3 ''Emma's Garden.''

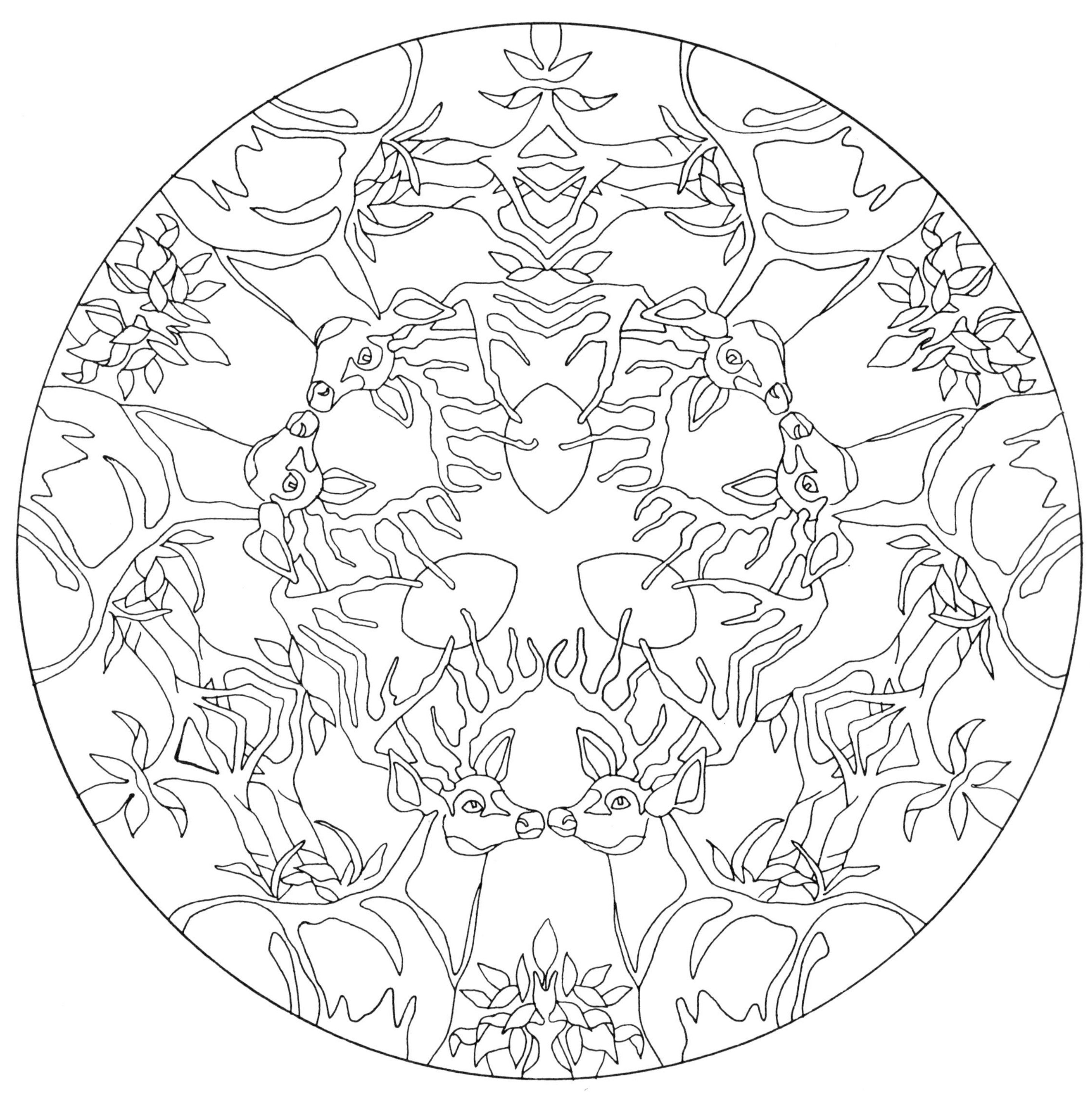

PLATE 4 ''Papa's Pet.''

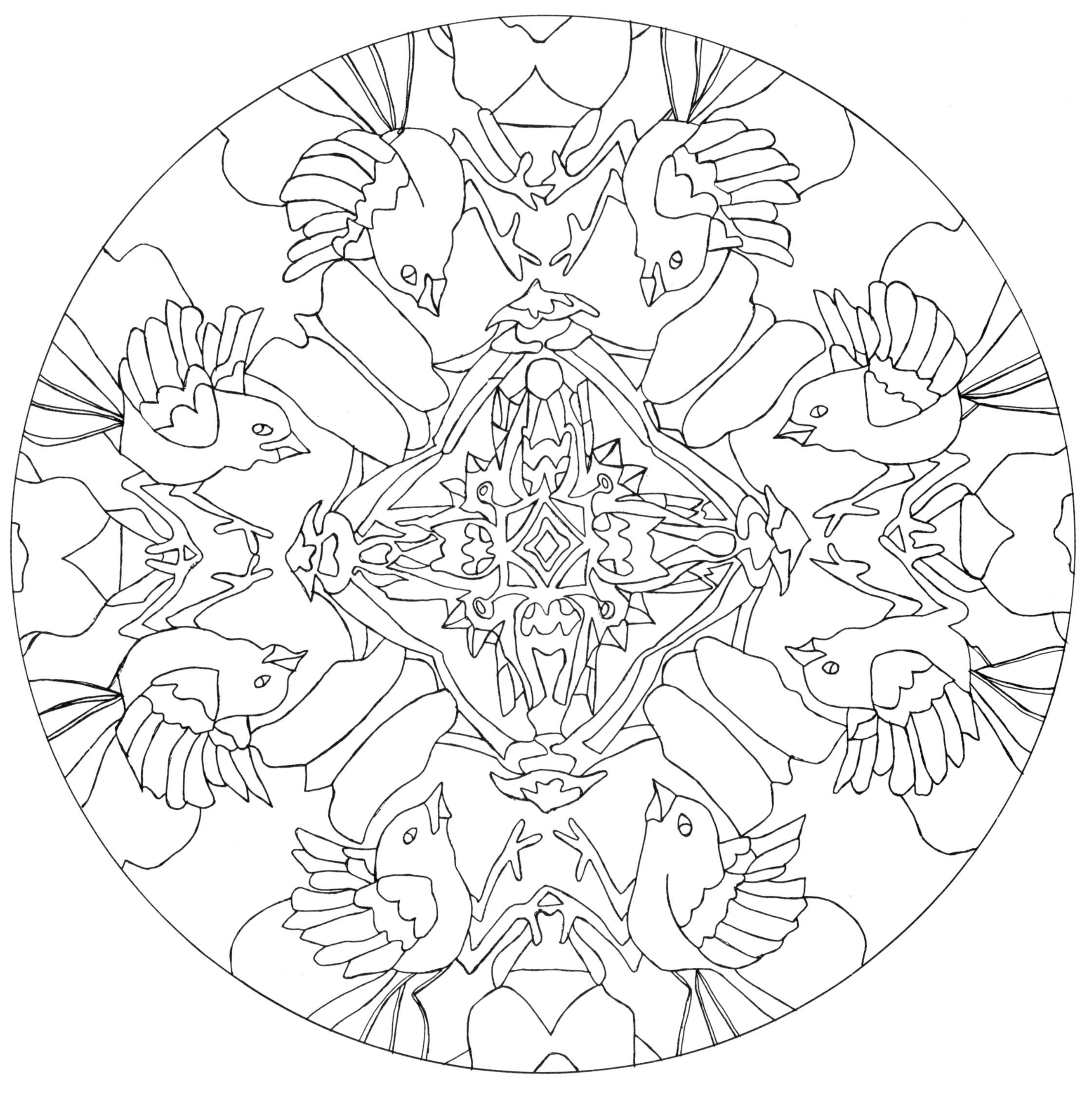

PLATE 5 "Bluebird."

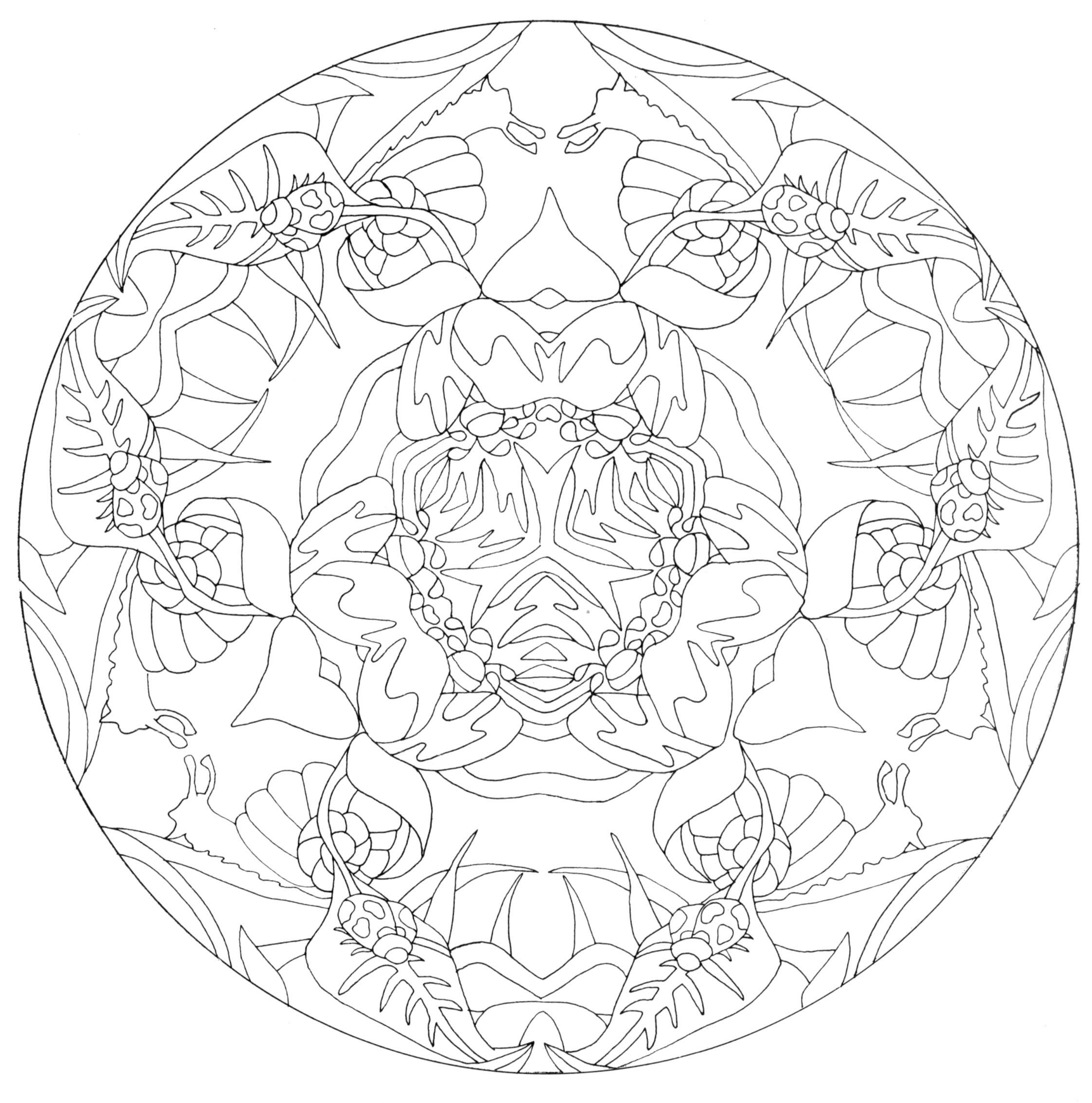

PLATE 6 "Ladybug and Friend."

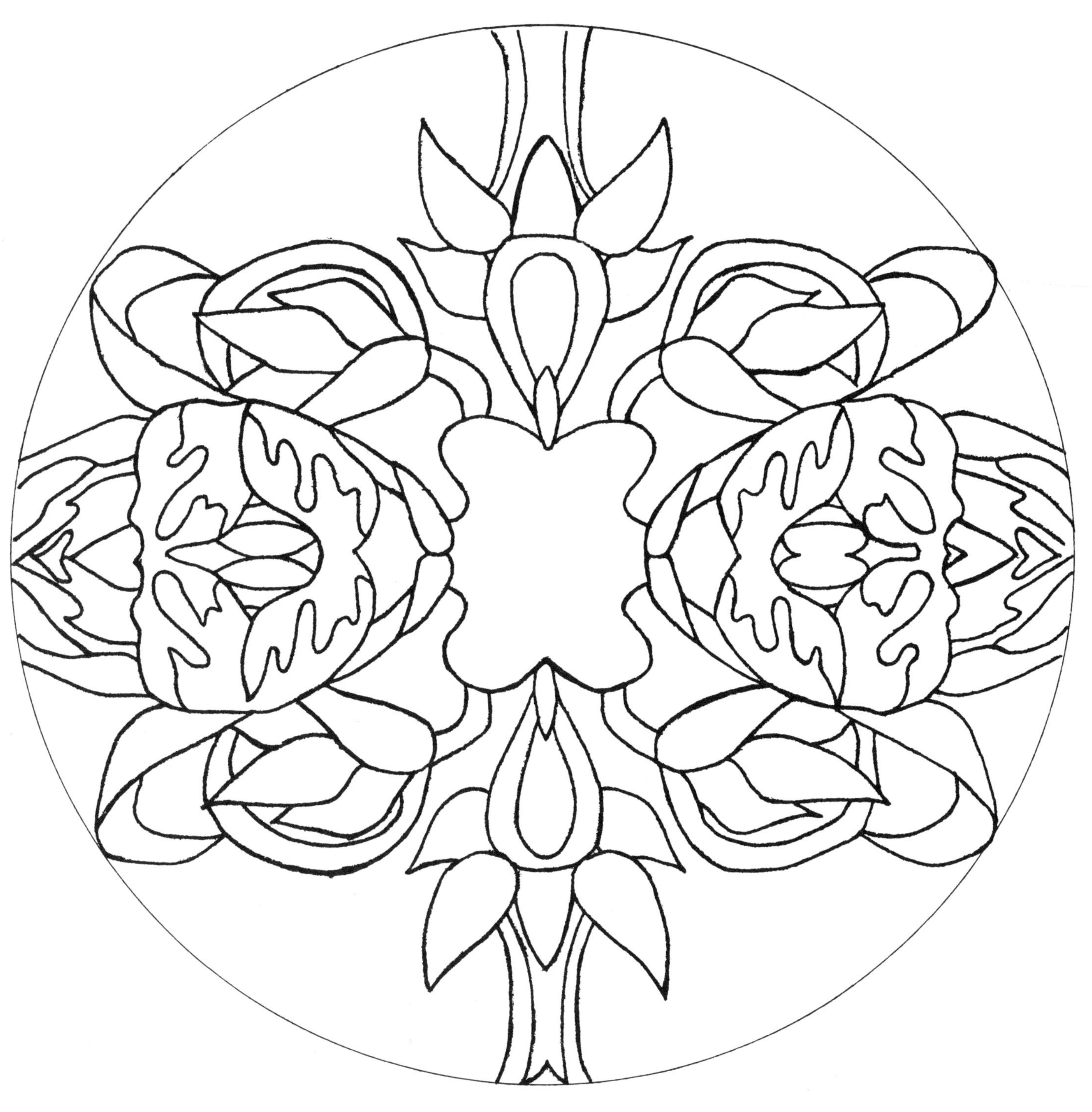

PLATE 7 "Small Floral Design."

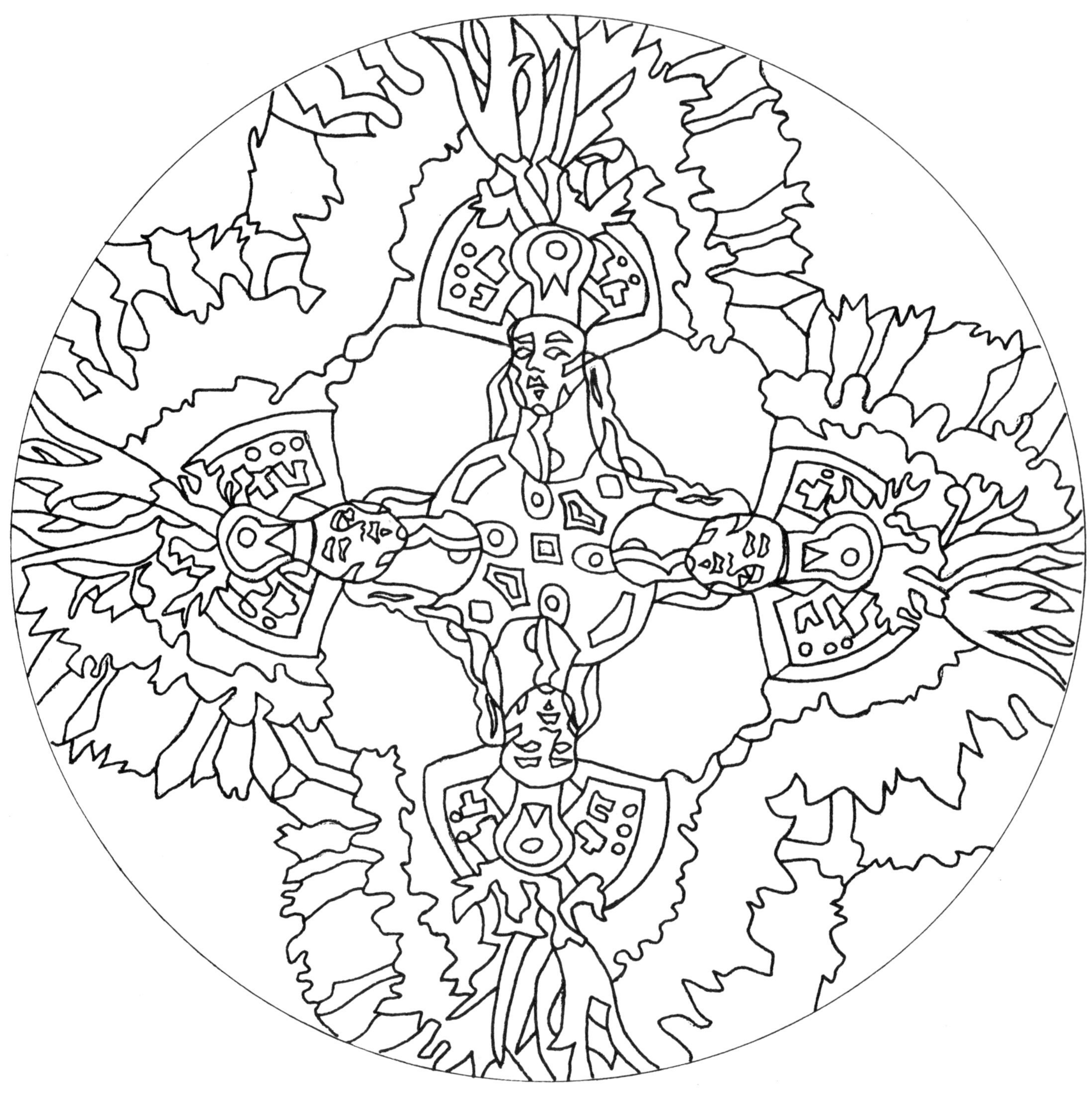

PLATE 8 "Aztec Indians."

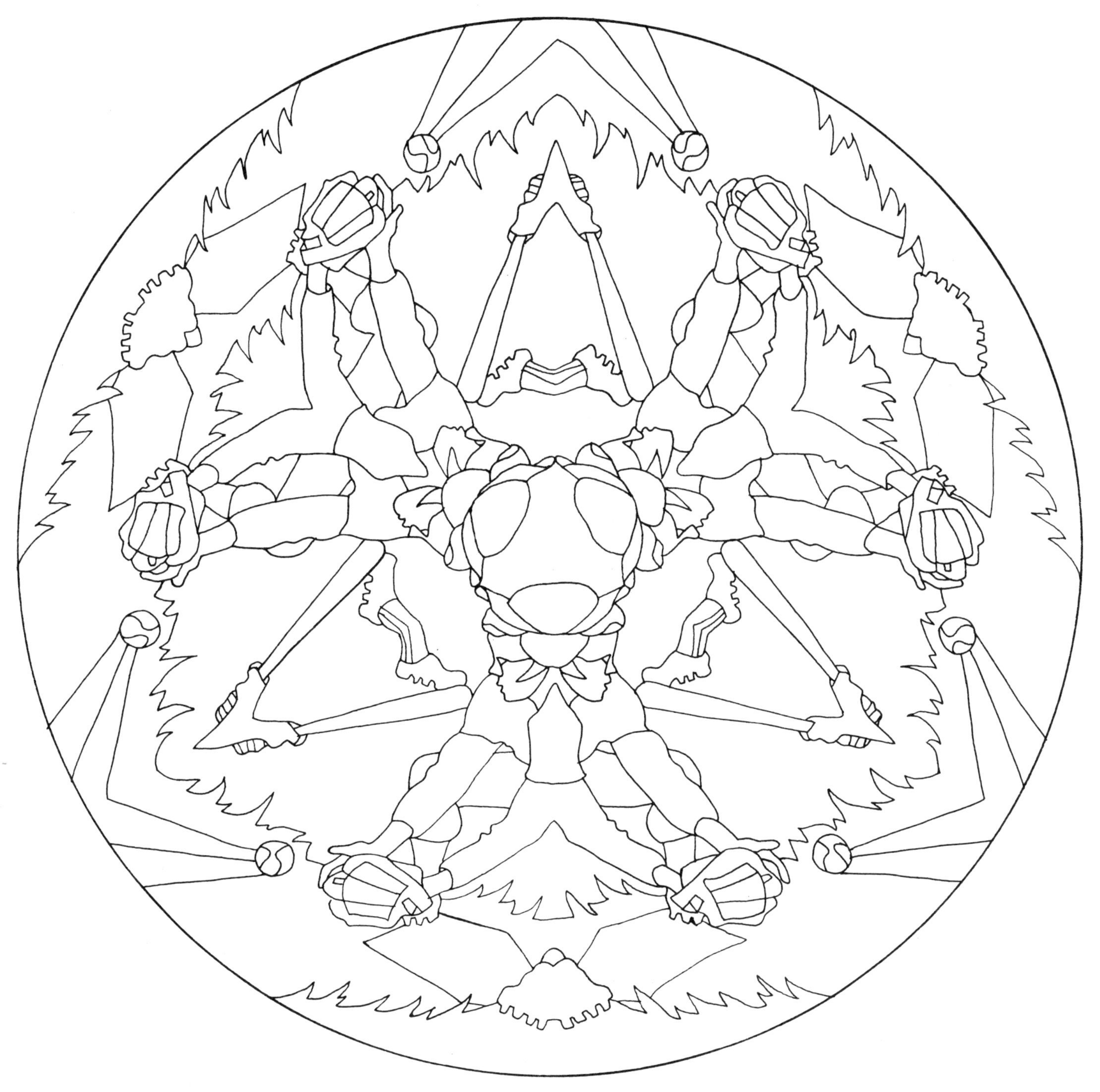

PLATE 9 "Play Ball."

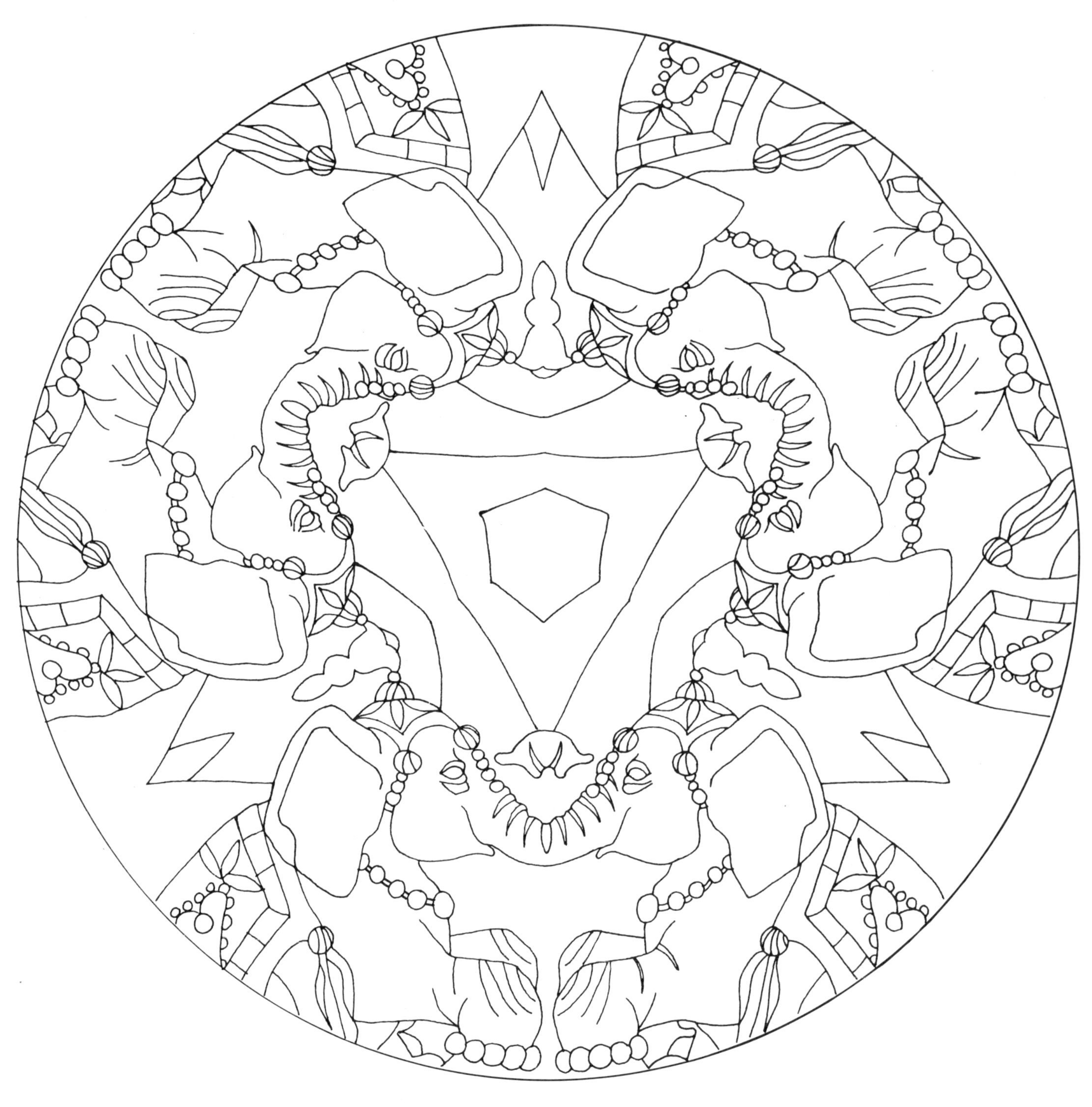

PLATE 10 "Elephant Walk."

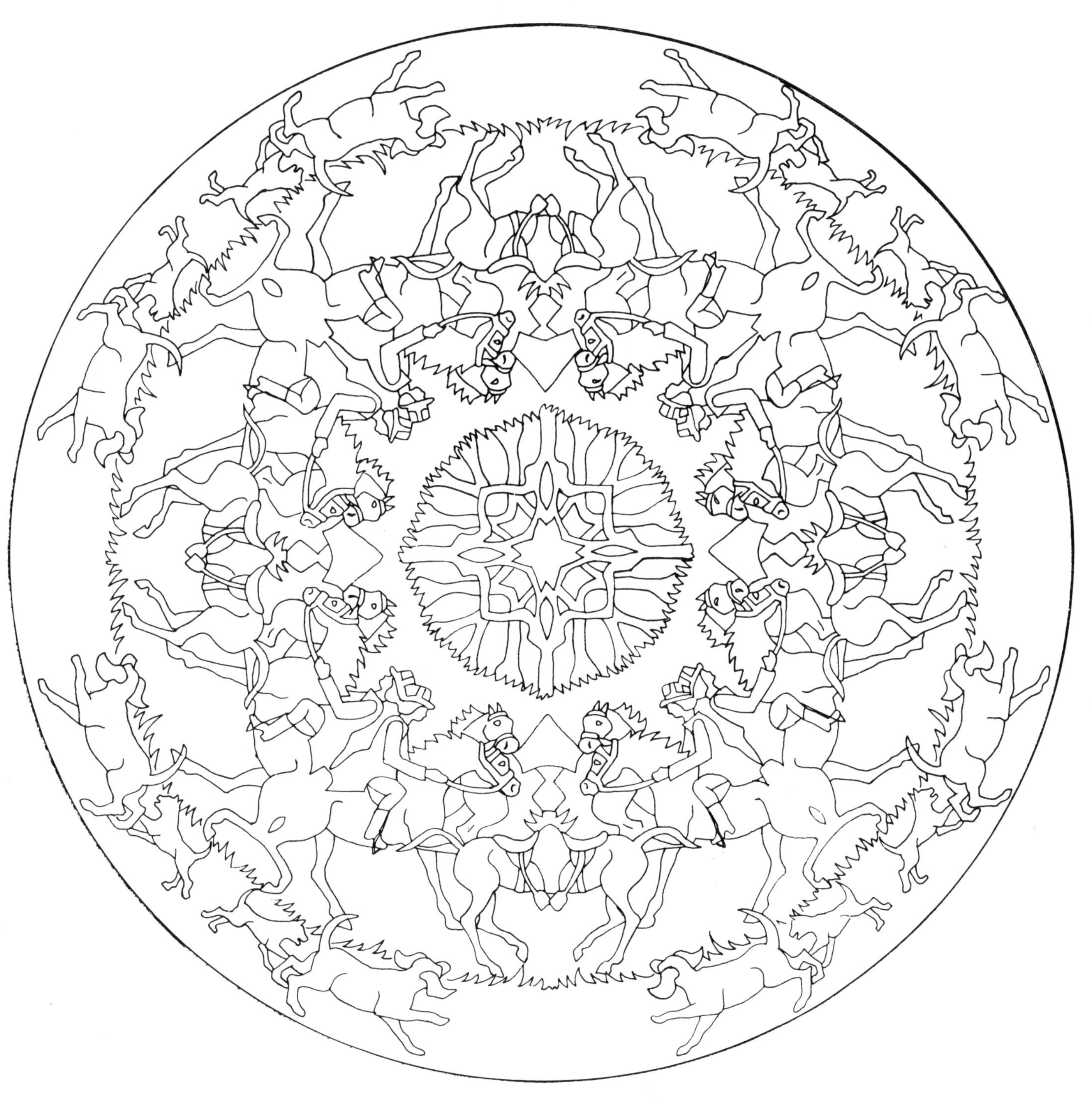

PLATE 11 "An Equestrienne's Dream."

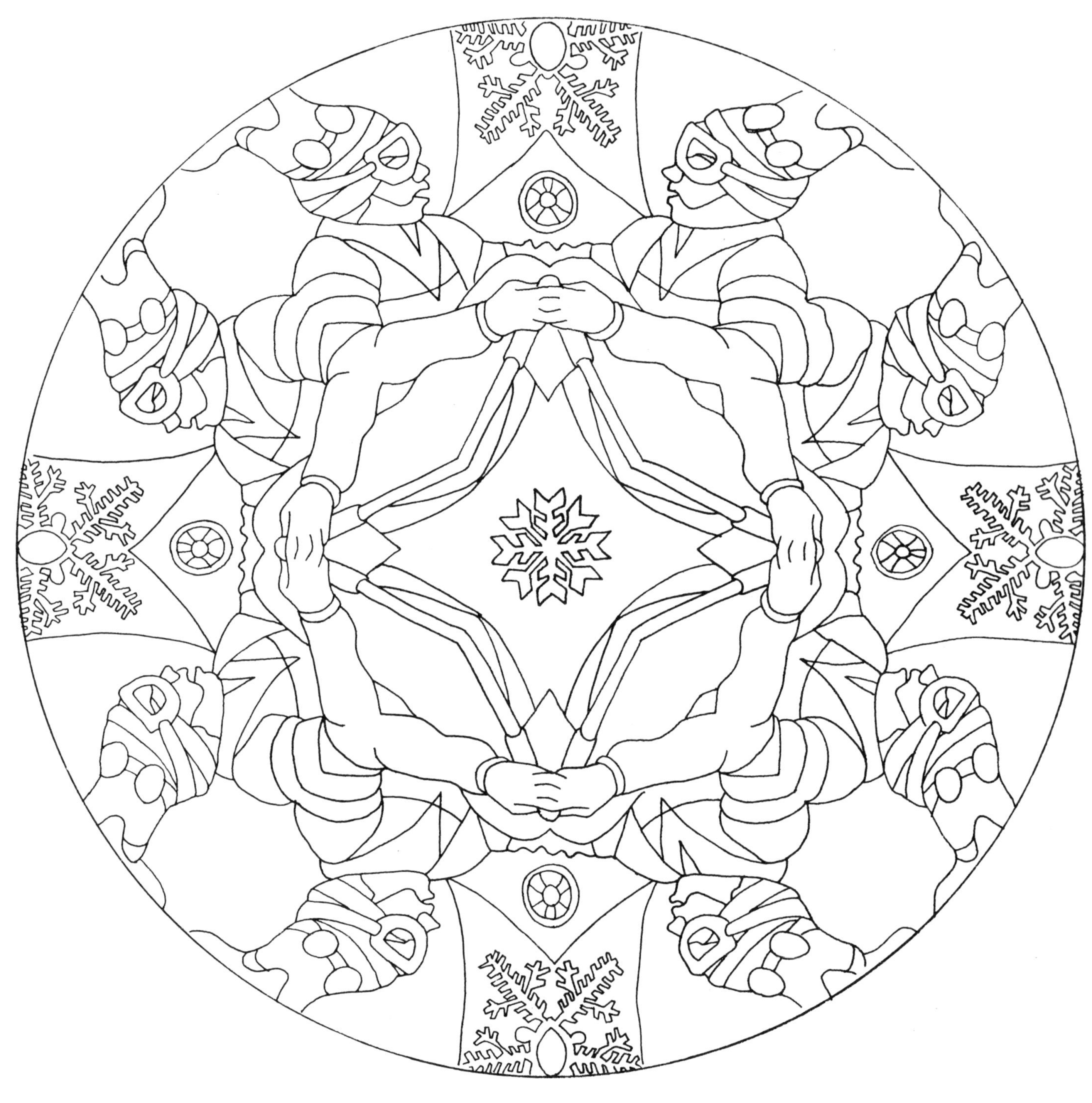

PLATE 12 "Think Snow."

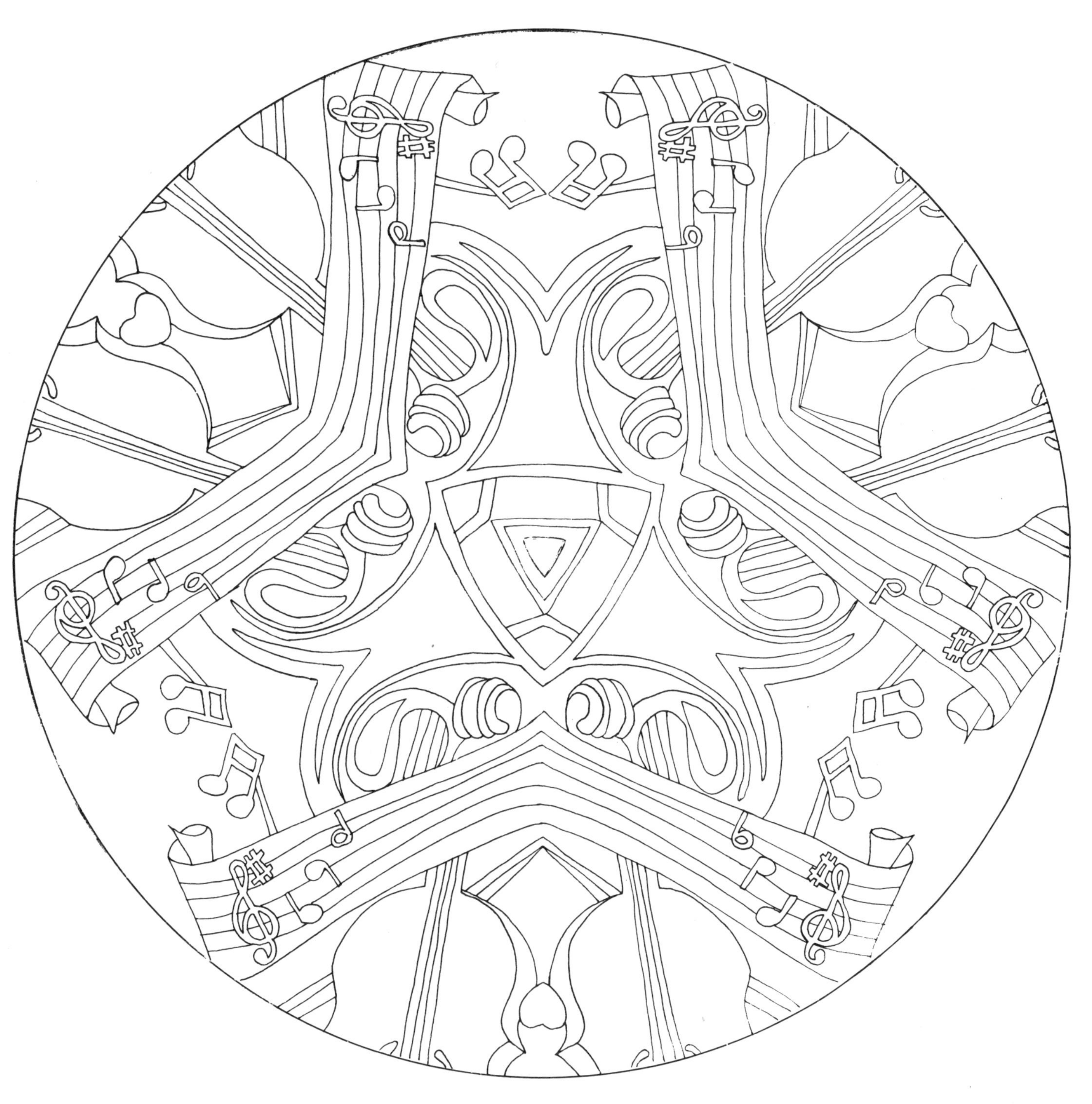

PLATE 13 "Do, Re, Mi."

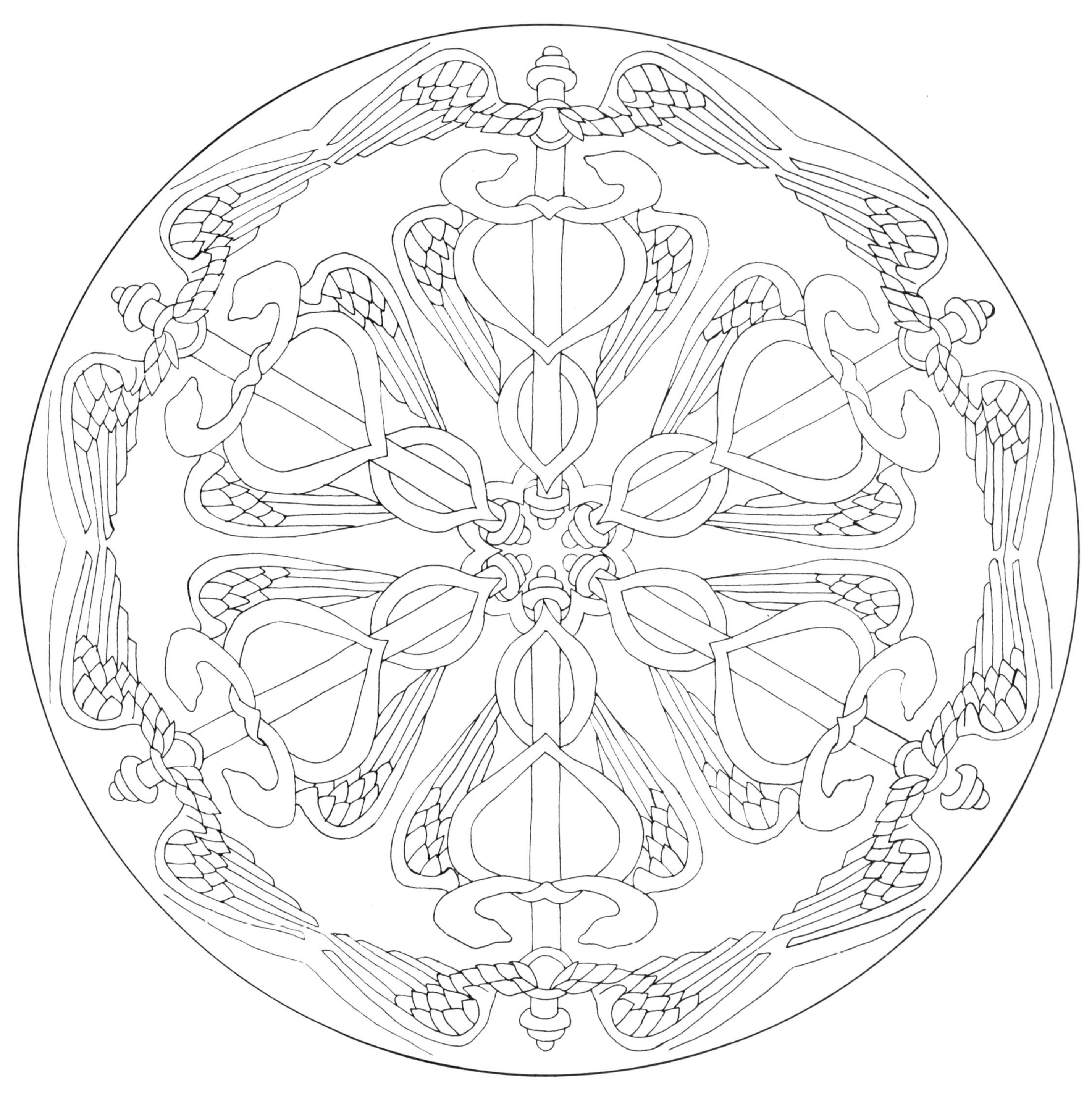

PLATE 14 "C. M. Z.'s Medical Art."

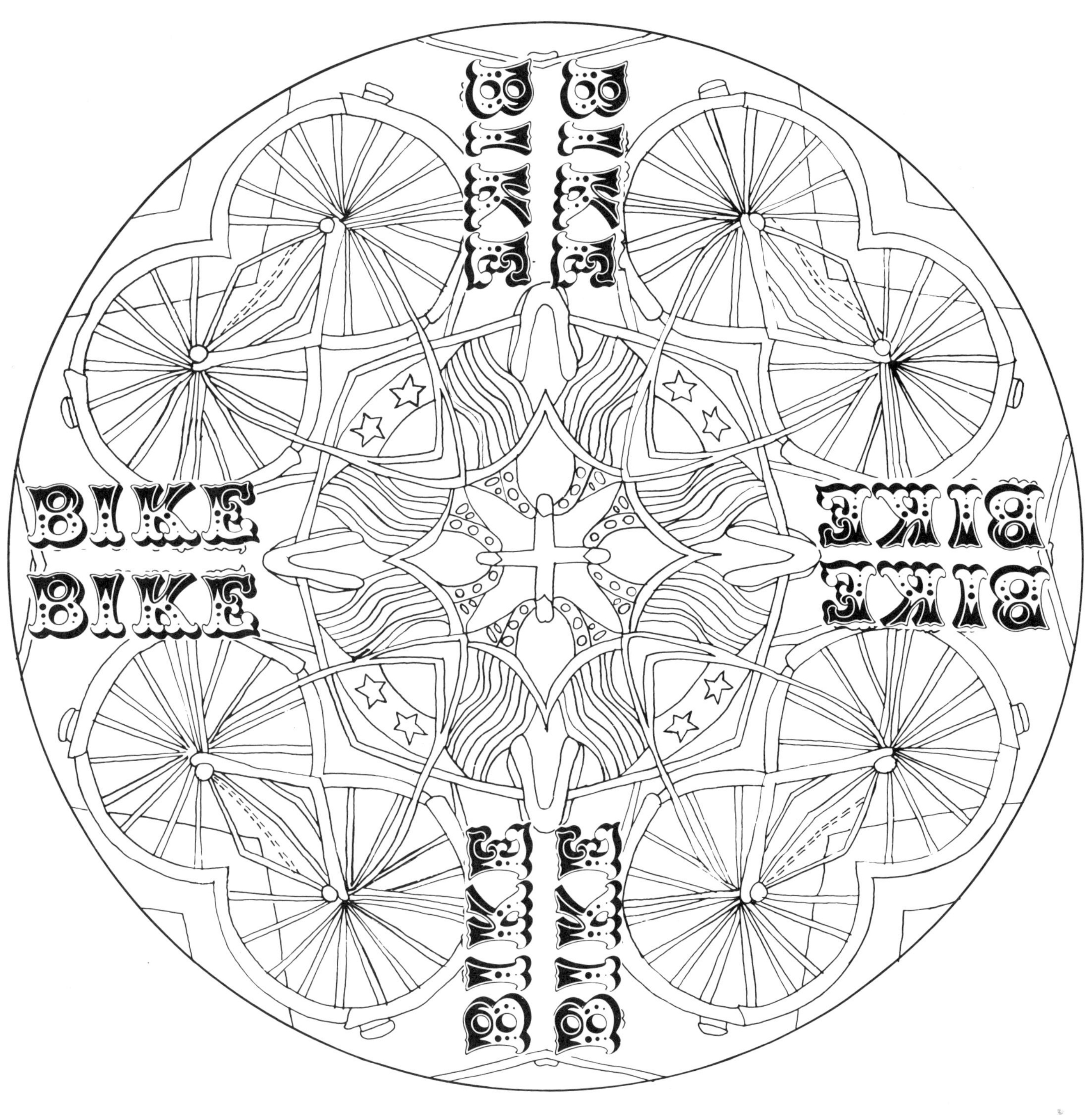

PLATE 15 "Bike."

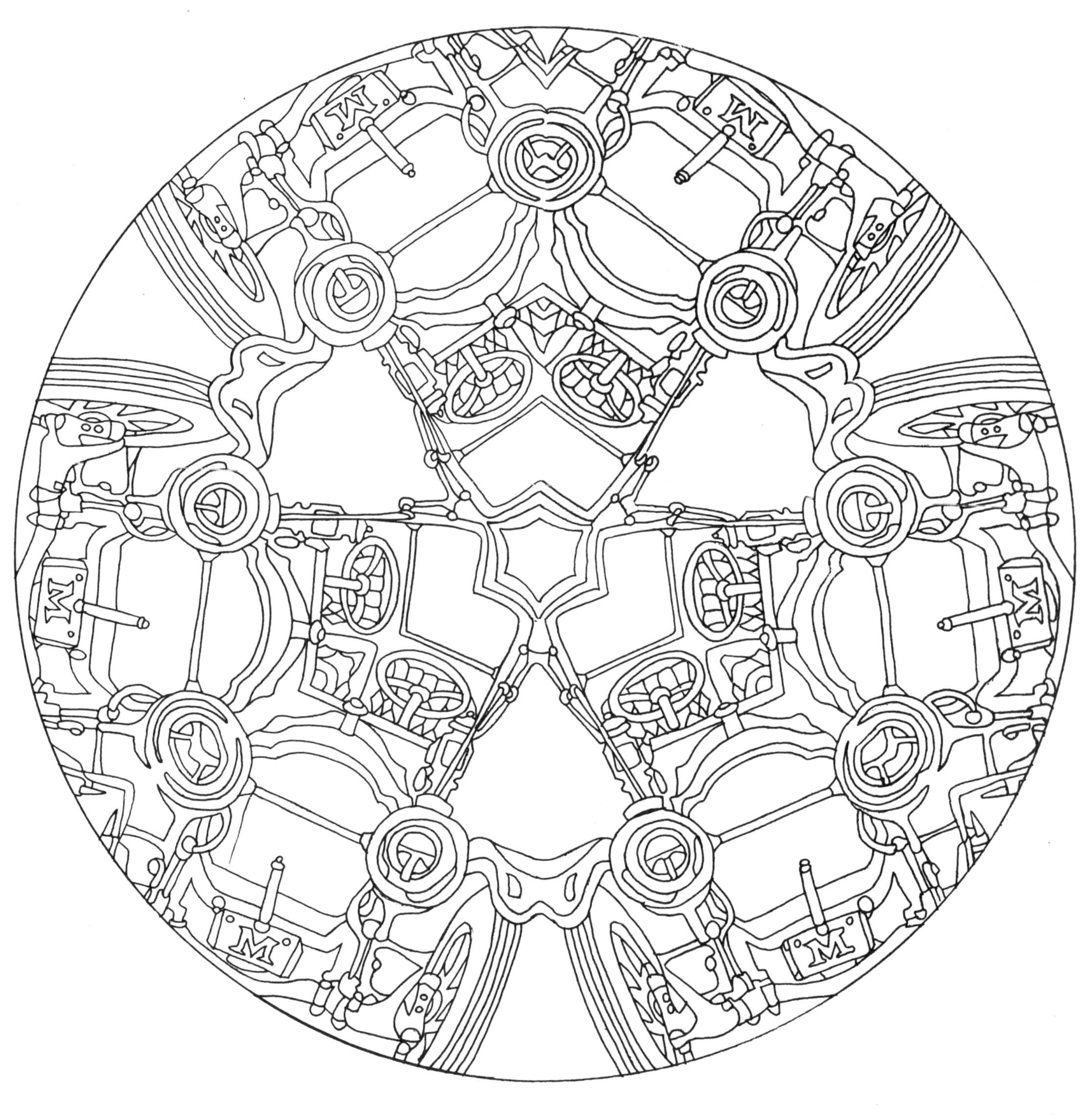

PLATE 16 ''Modesto's Dream.''

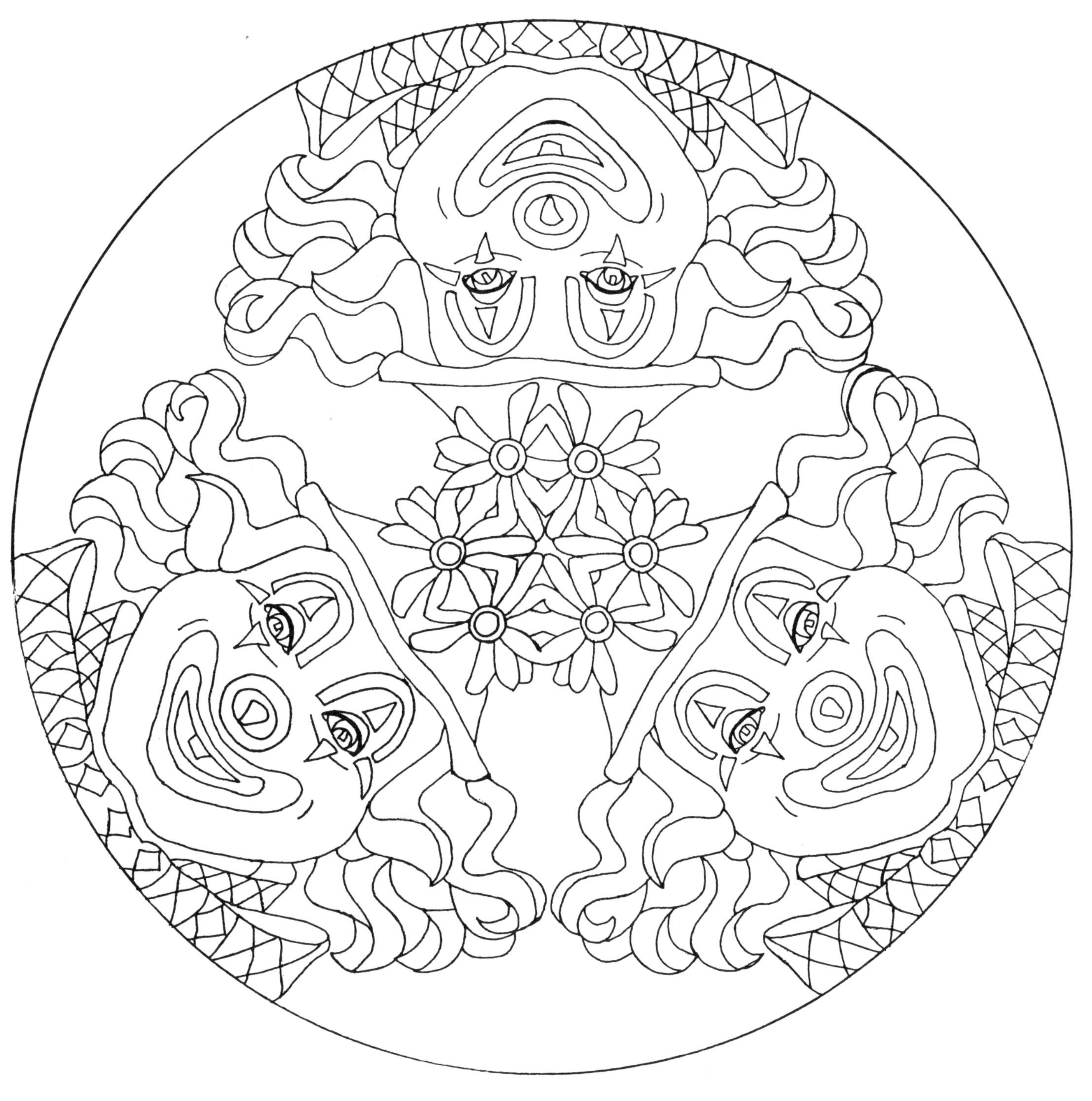

PLATE 17 "Funny Face."

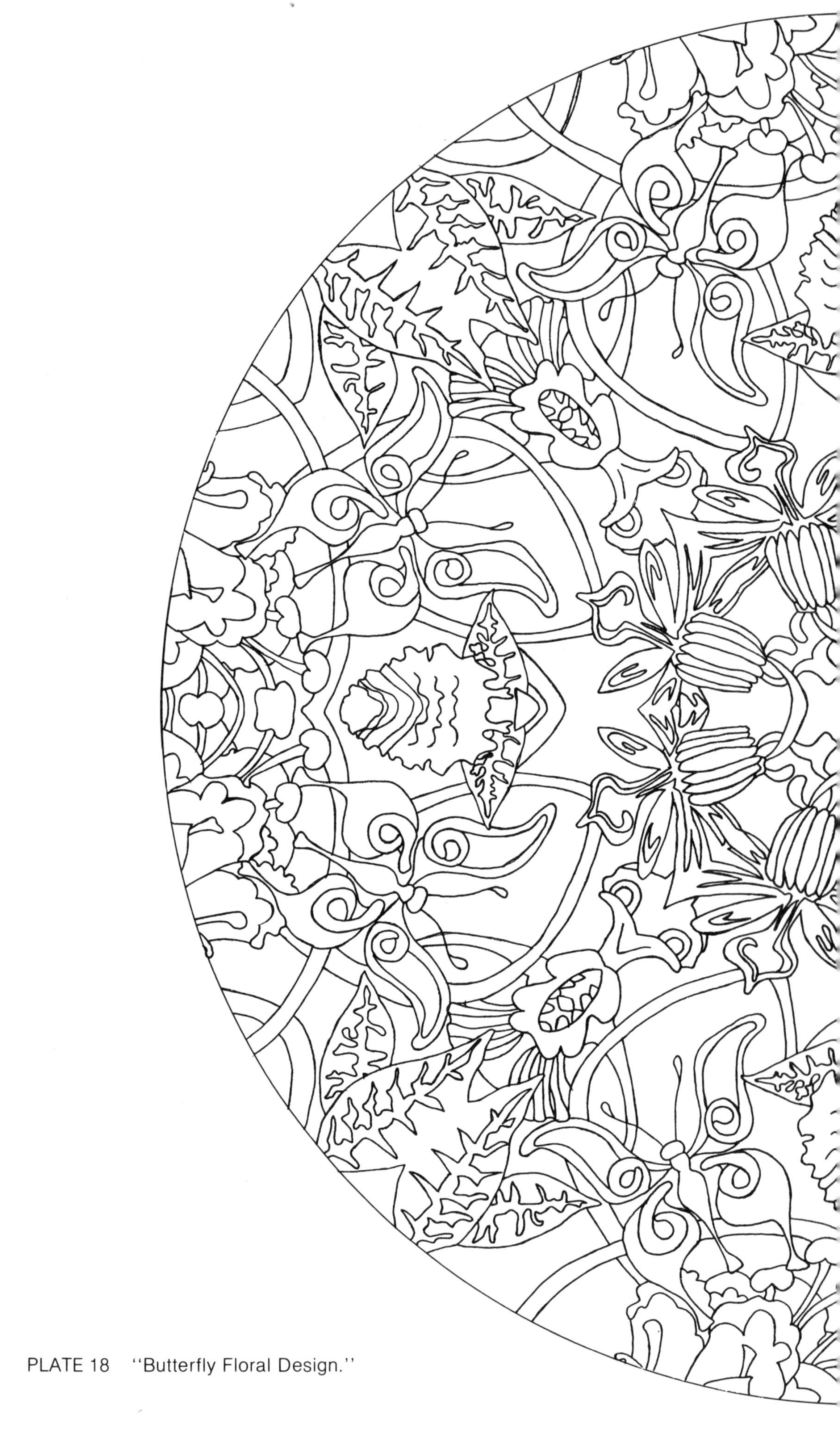

PLATE 18 "Butterfly Floral Design."

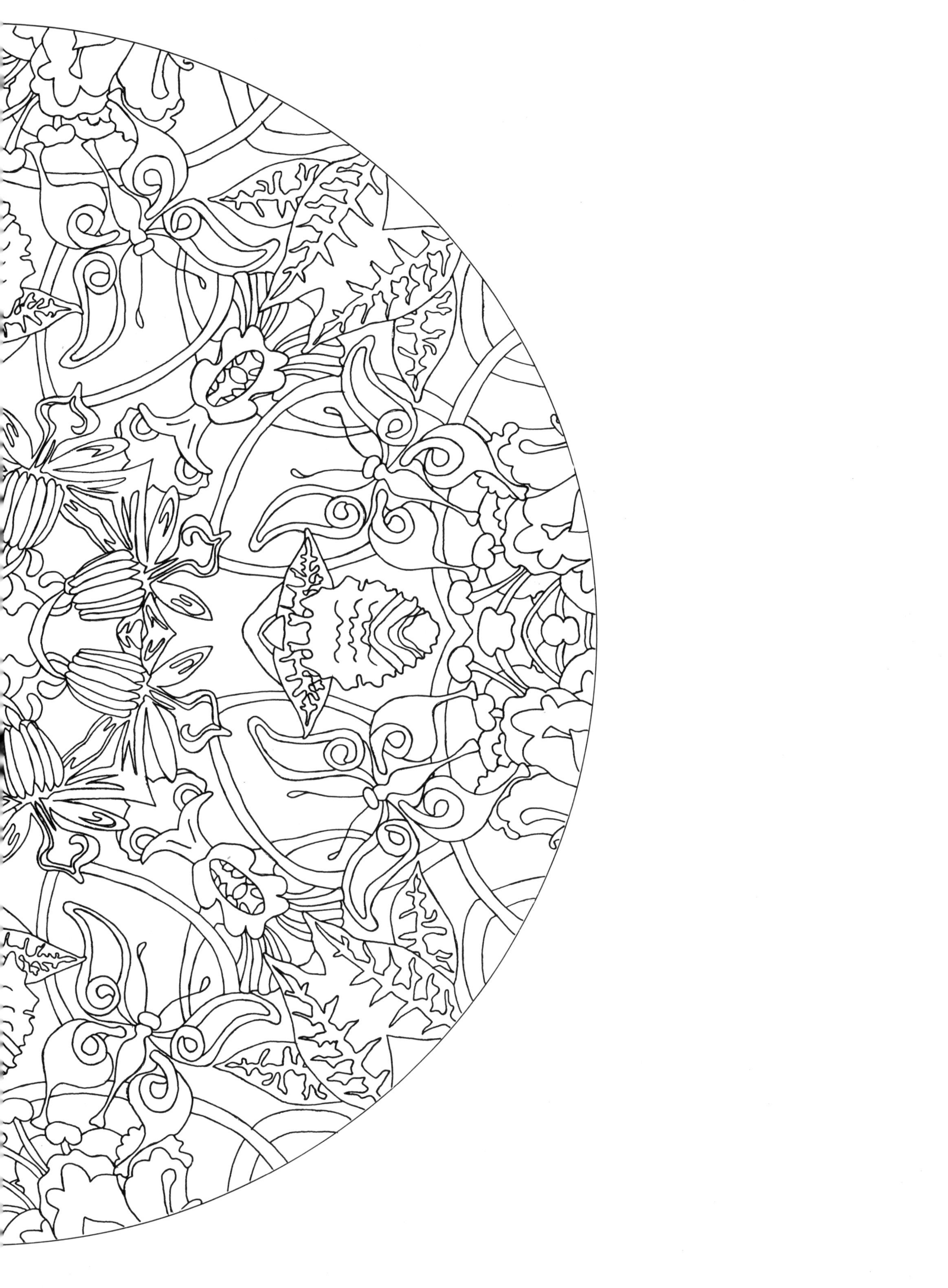

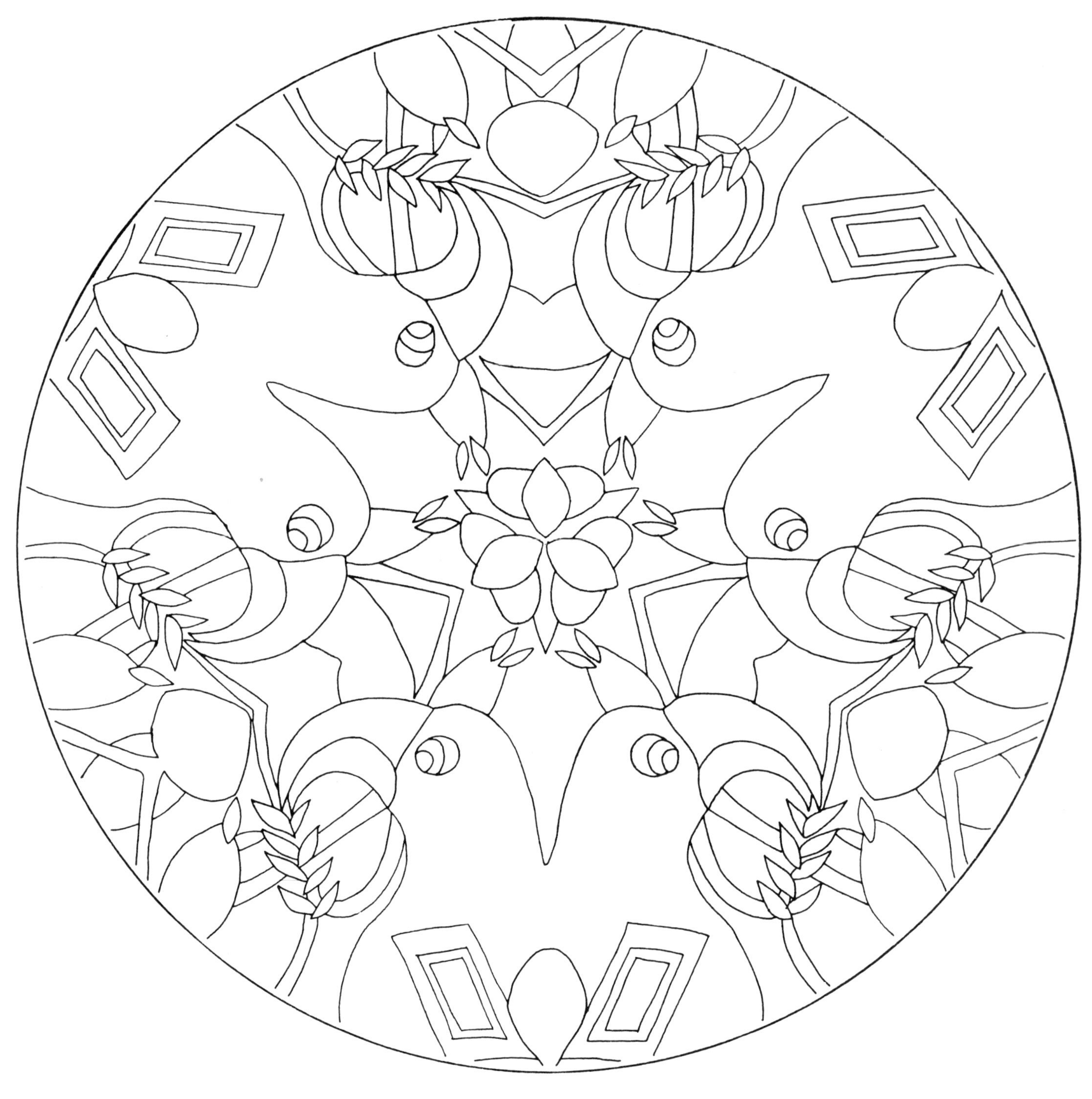

PLATE 19 “Pájaros.”

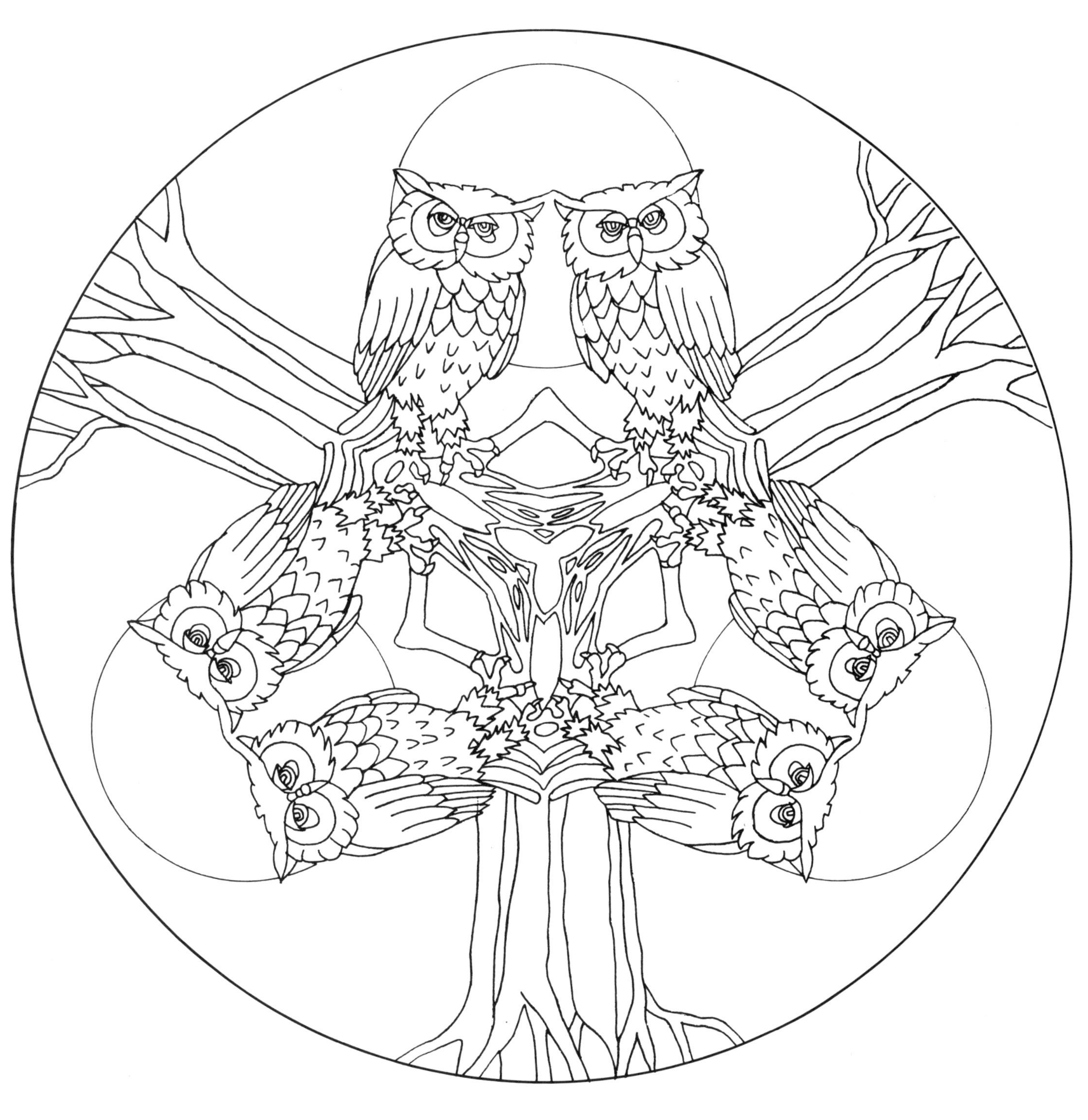

PLATE 20 "Marion's Pets."

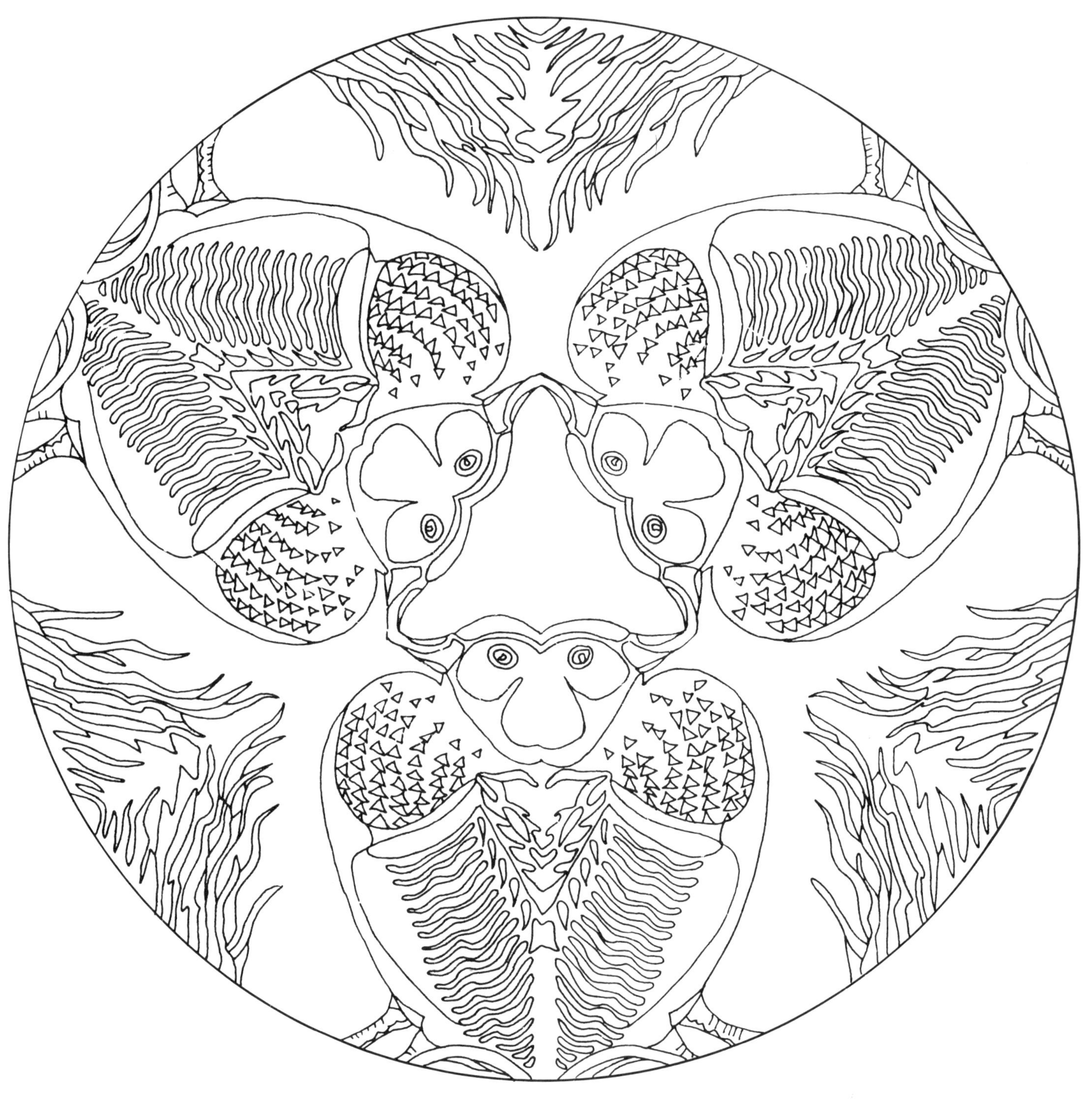

PLATE 21 "Green's Sanctuary."

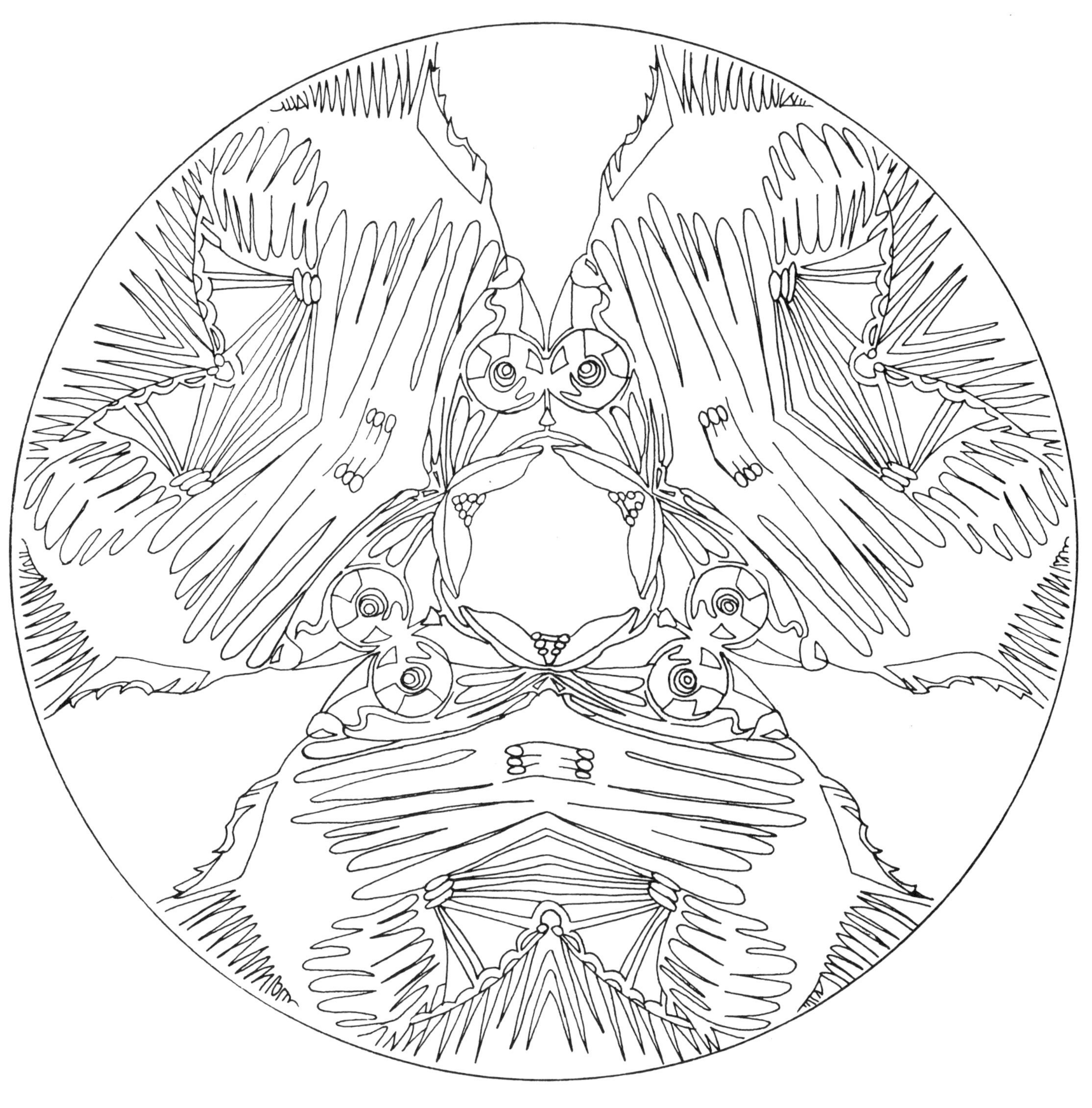

PLATE 22 "Sybil's Friend."

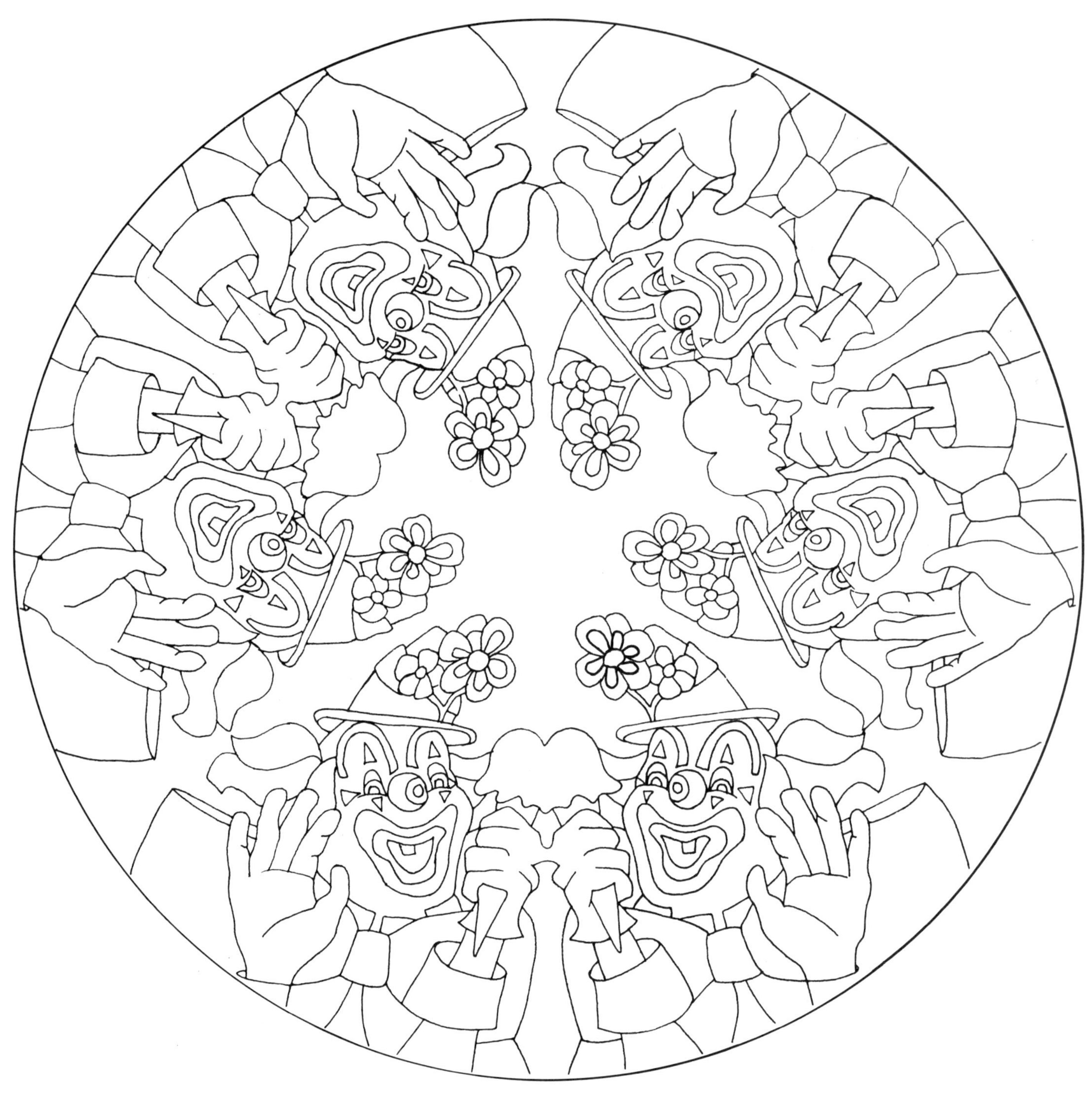

PLATE 23 "Ice Cream Time."

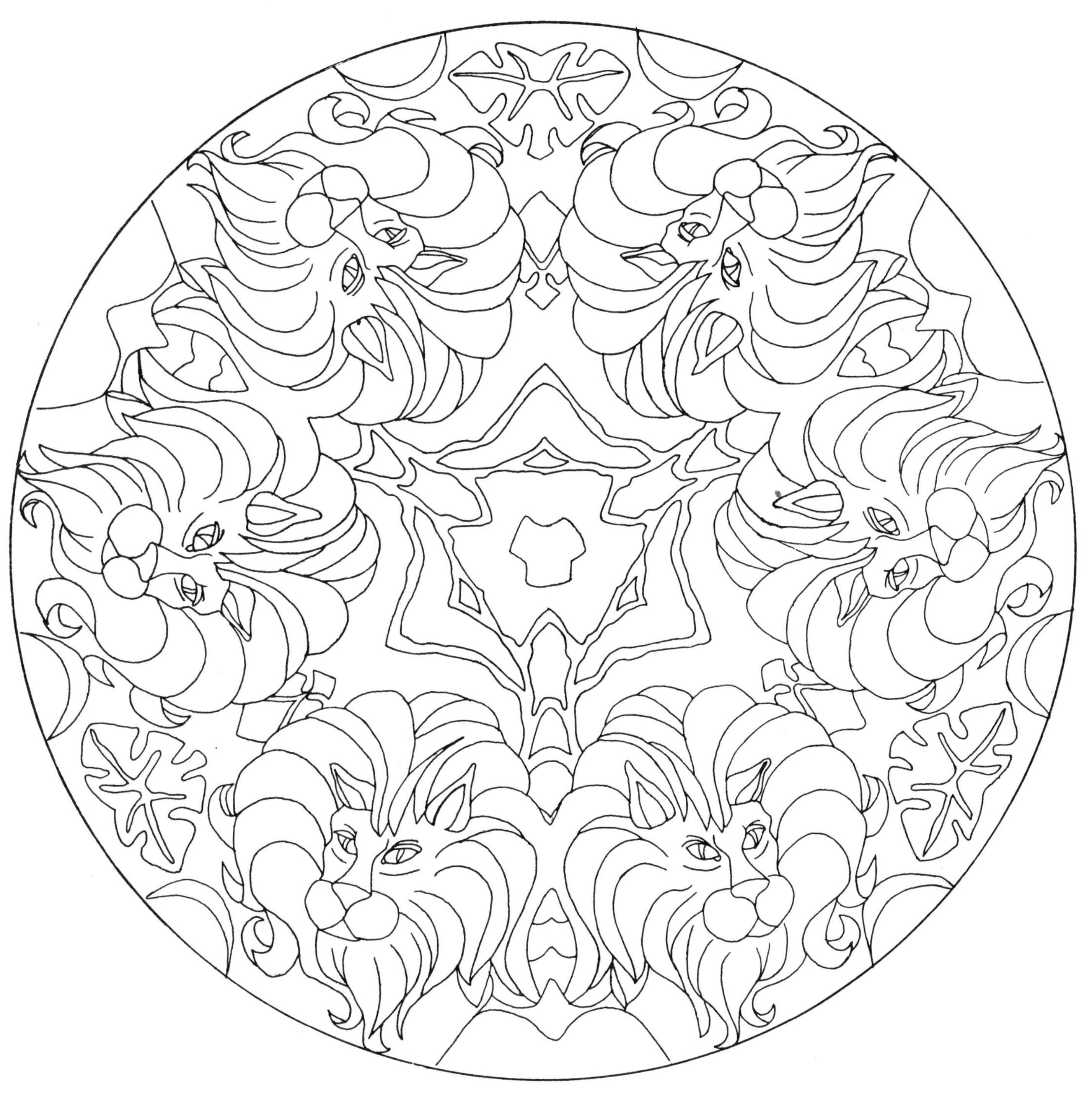

PLATE 24 "Bernice's Zodiac."

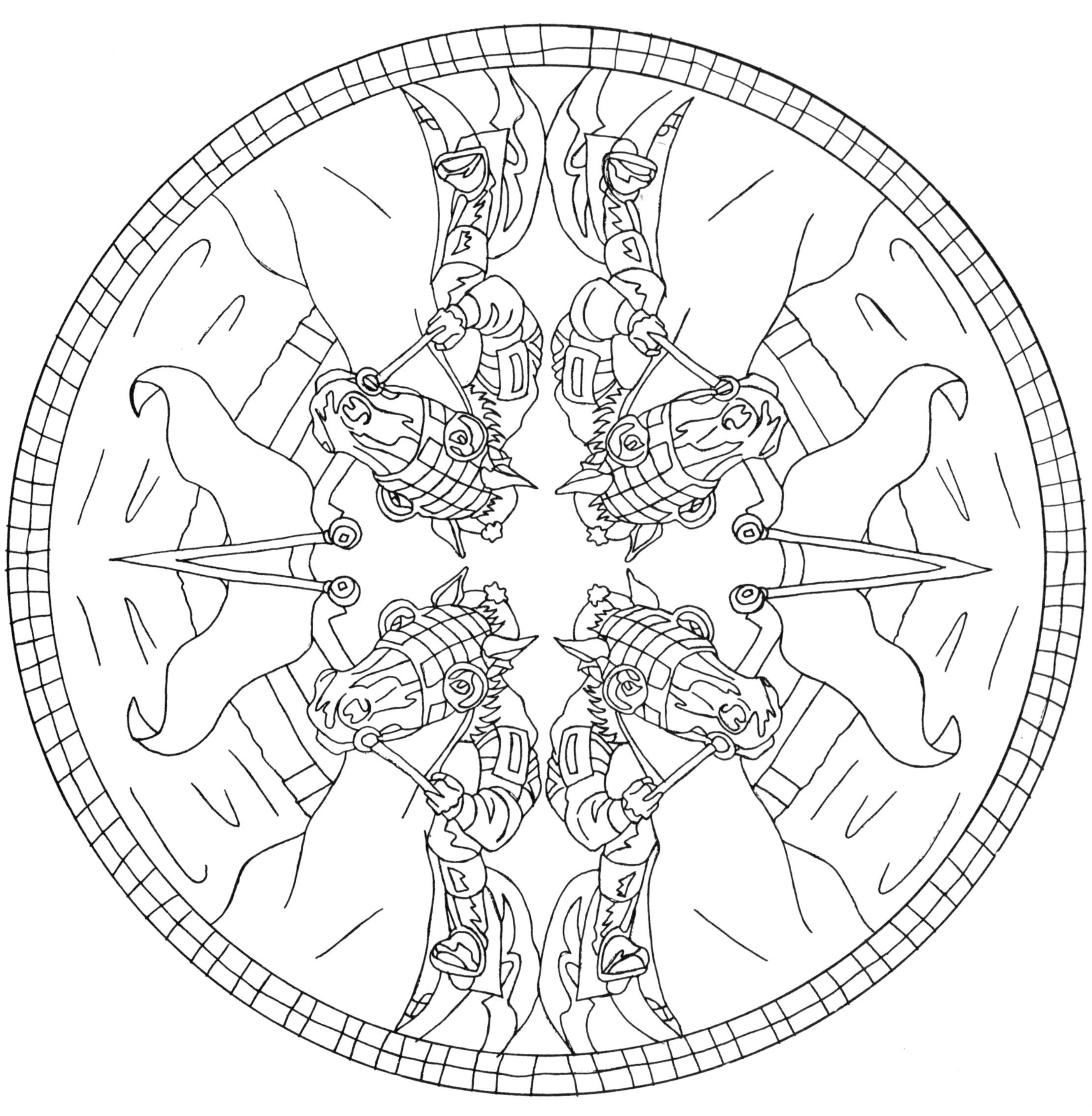

PLATE 25 "Nanny's Choice."

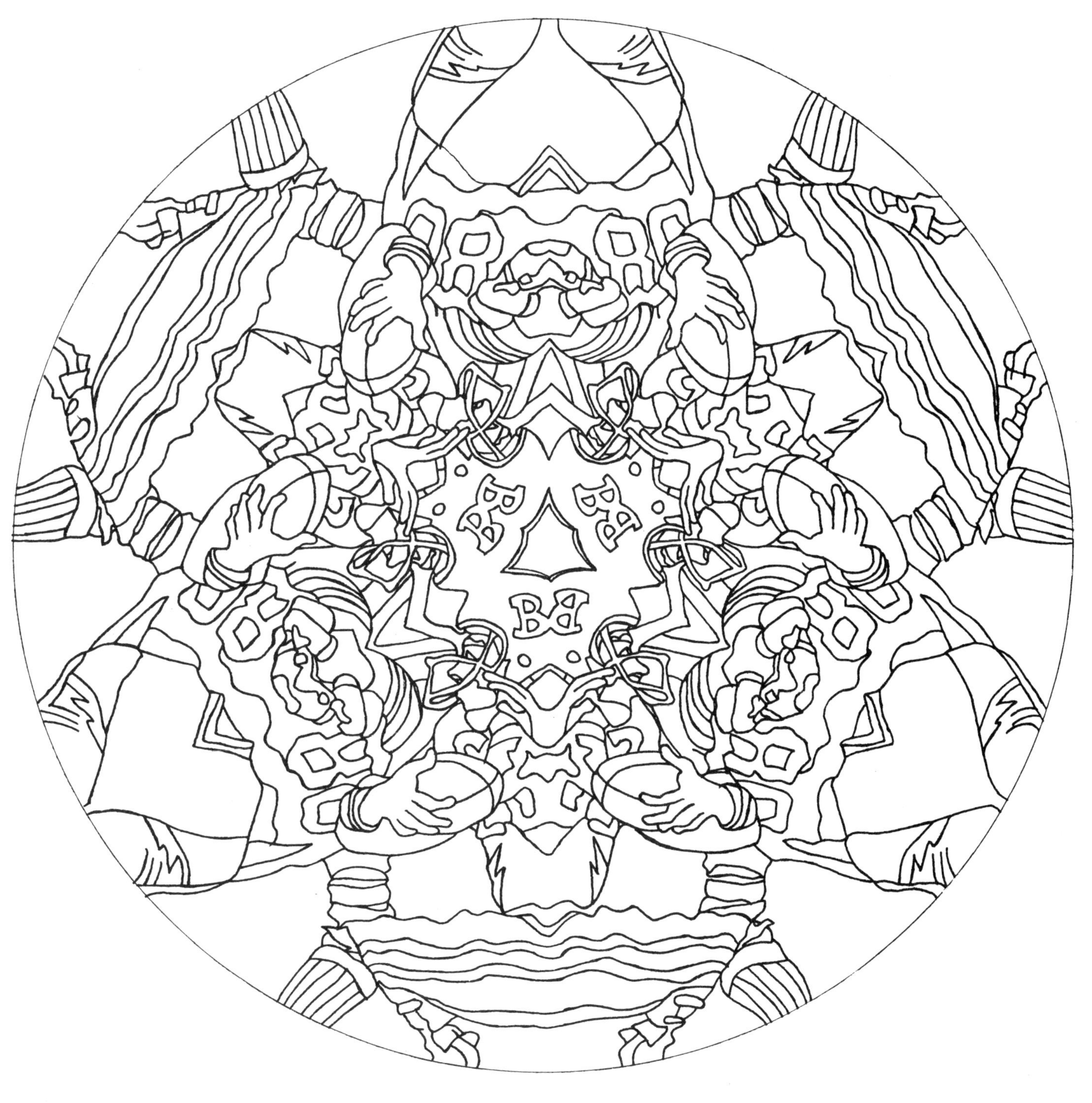

PLATE 26 ''Football in Action.''

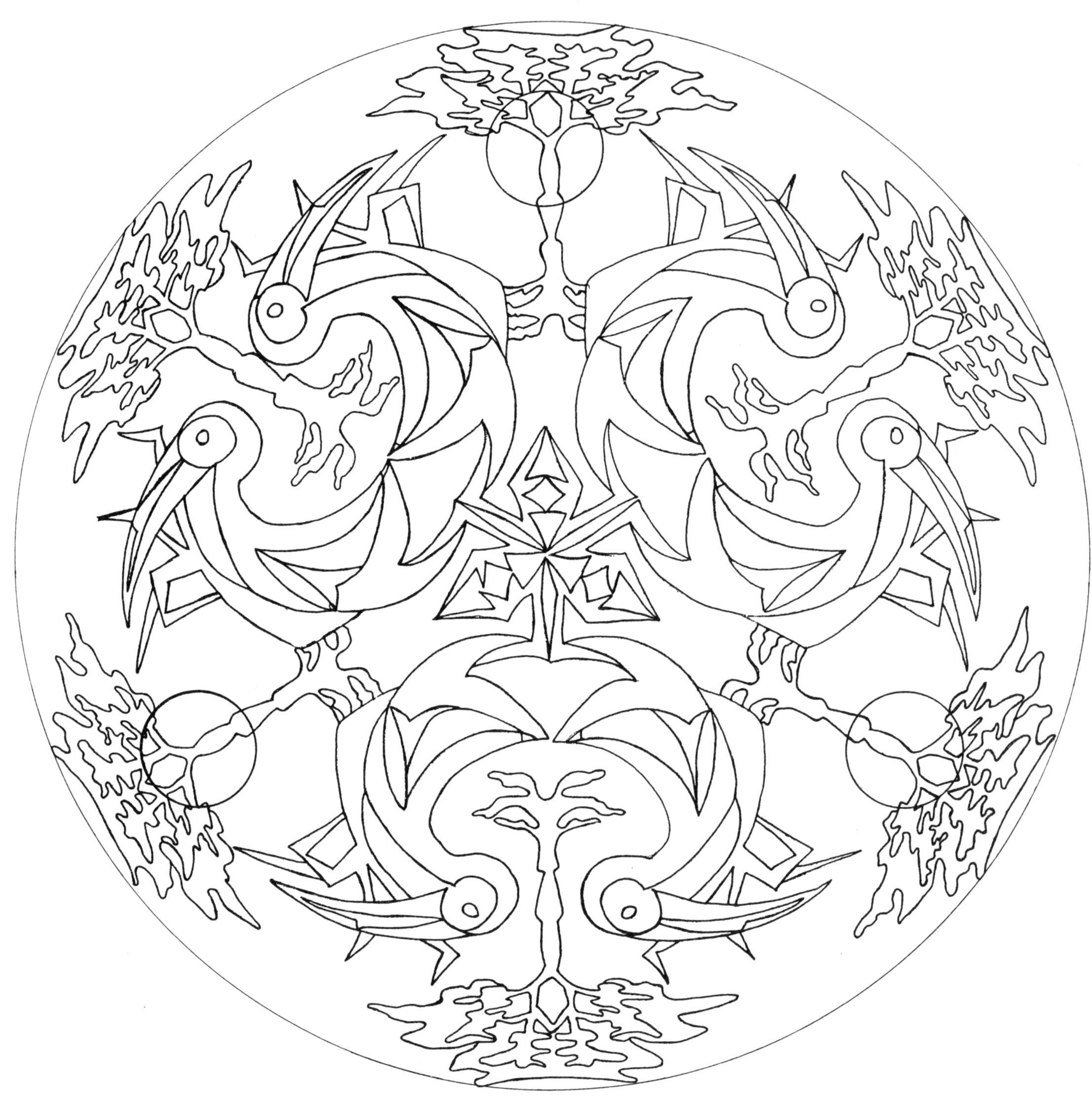

PLATE 27 ''African Roadrunner.''

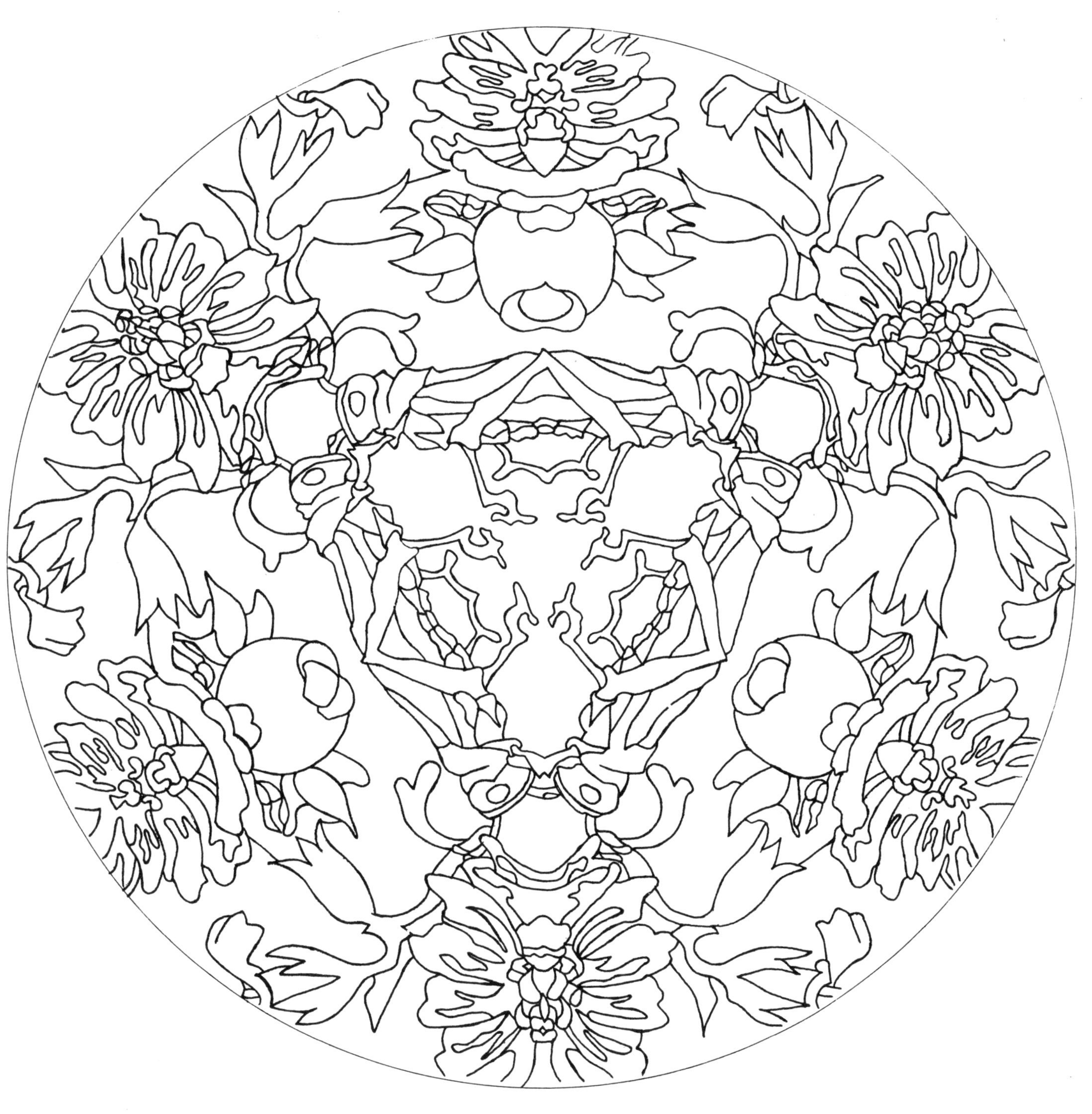

PLATE 28 ''Grasshoppers.''

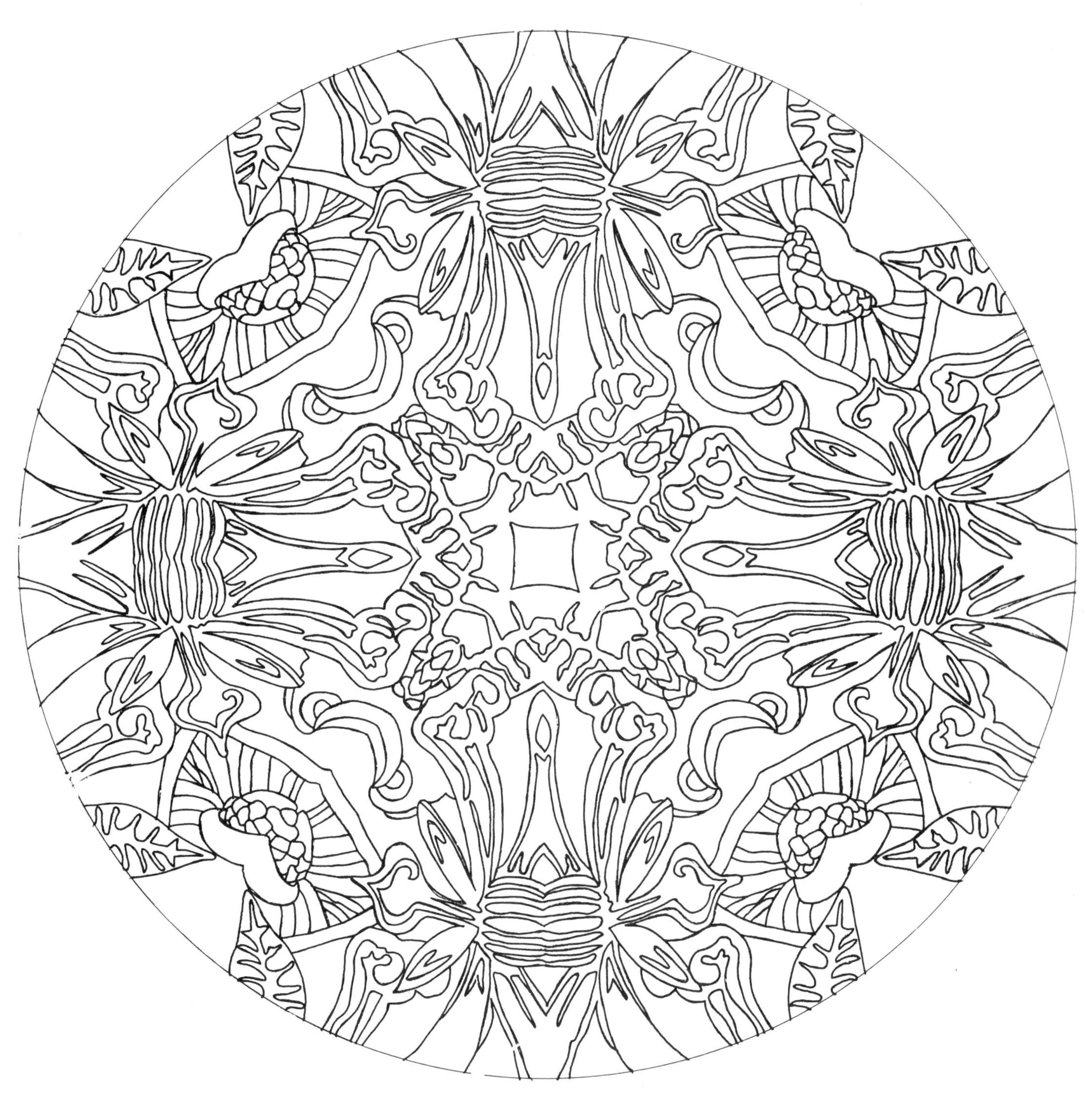

PLATE 29 "Floral Design."

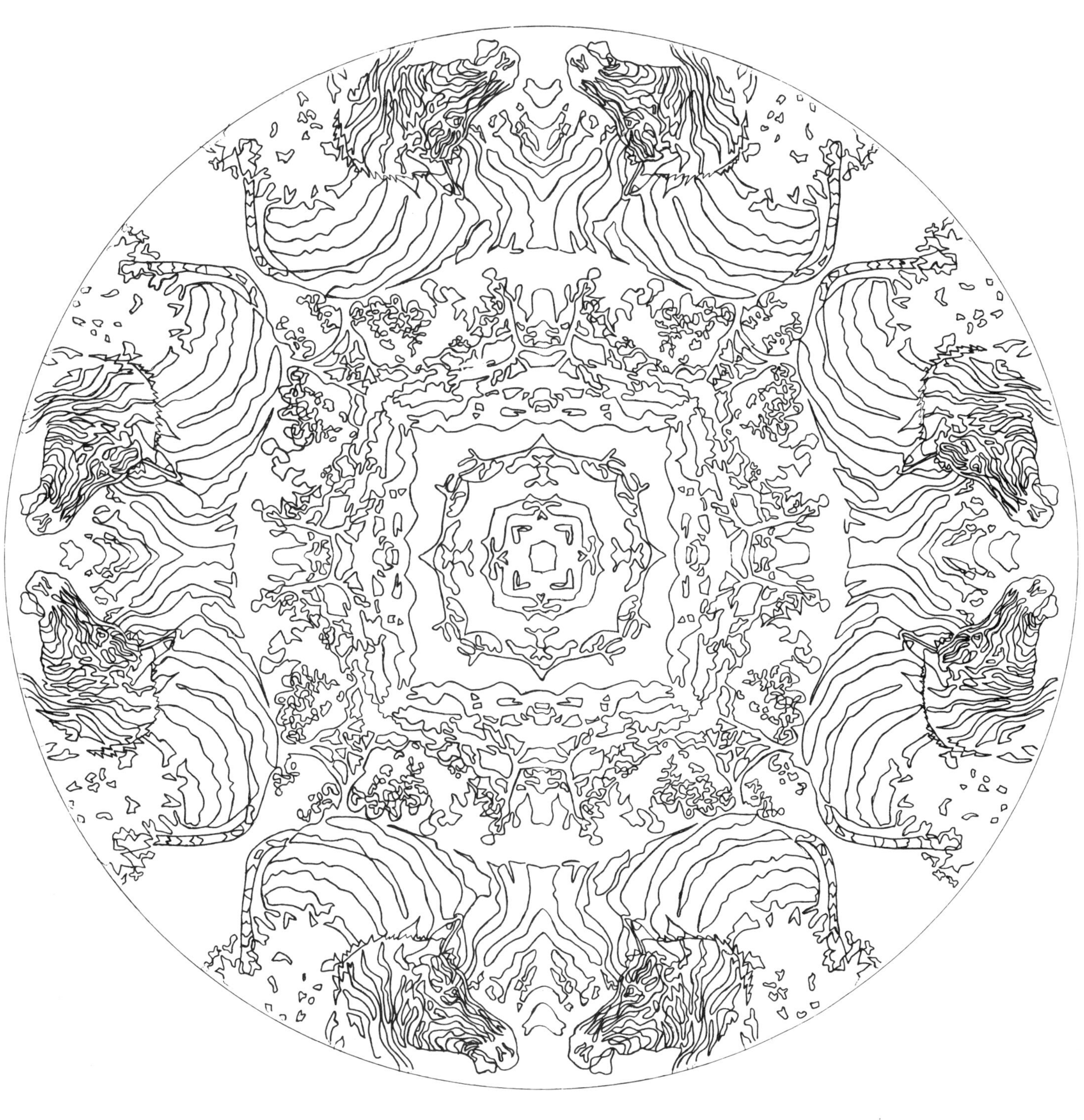

PLATE 30 "Zebra-Go-Round."

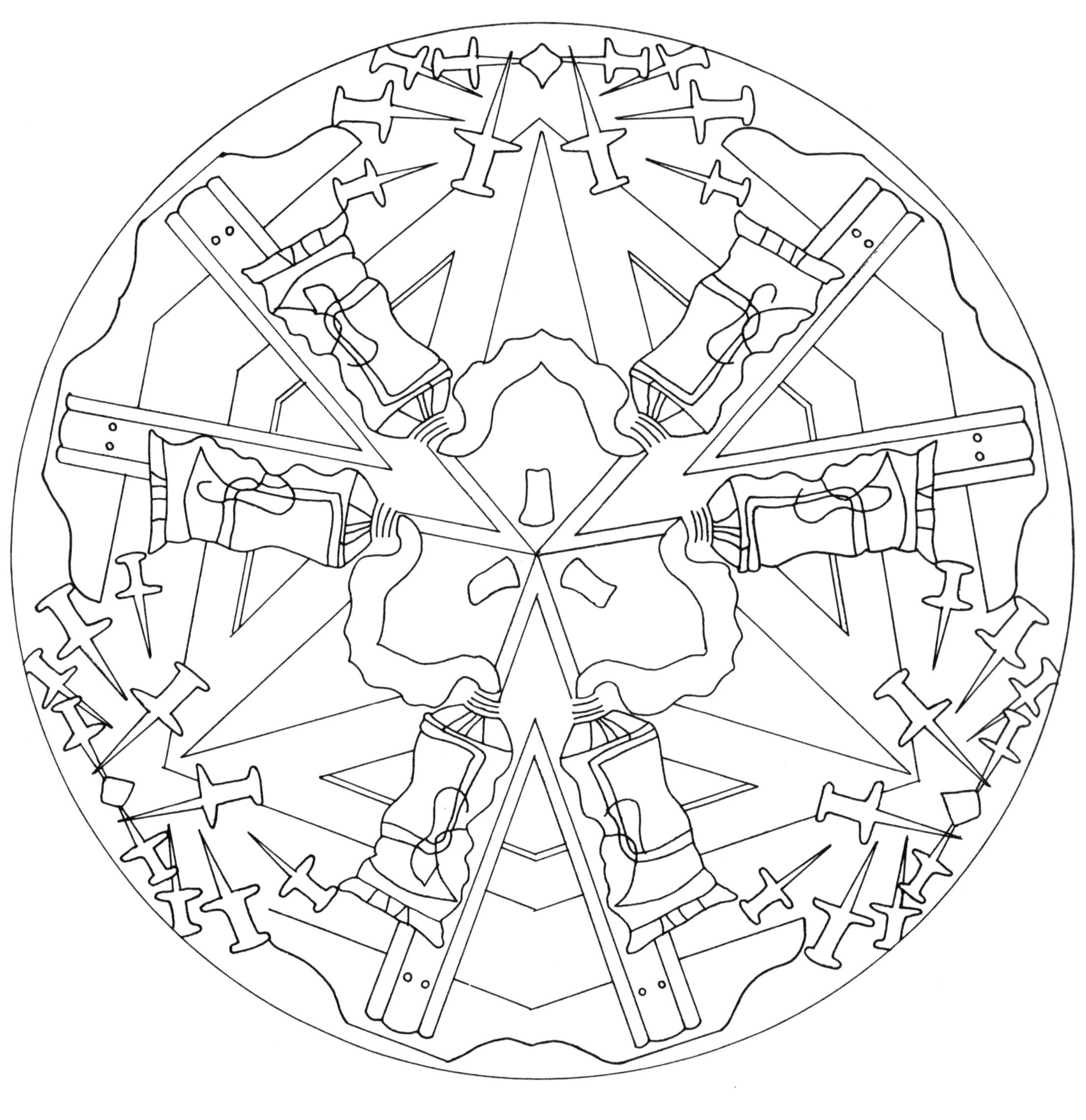

PLATE 31 "Artist's Dilemma."

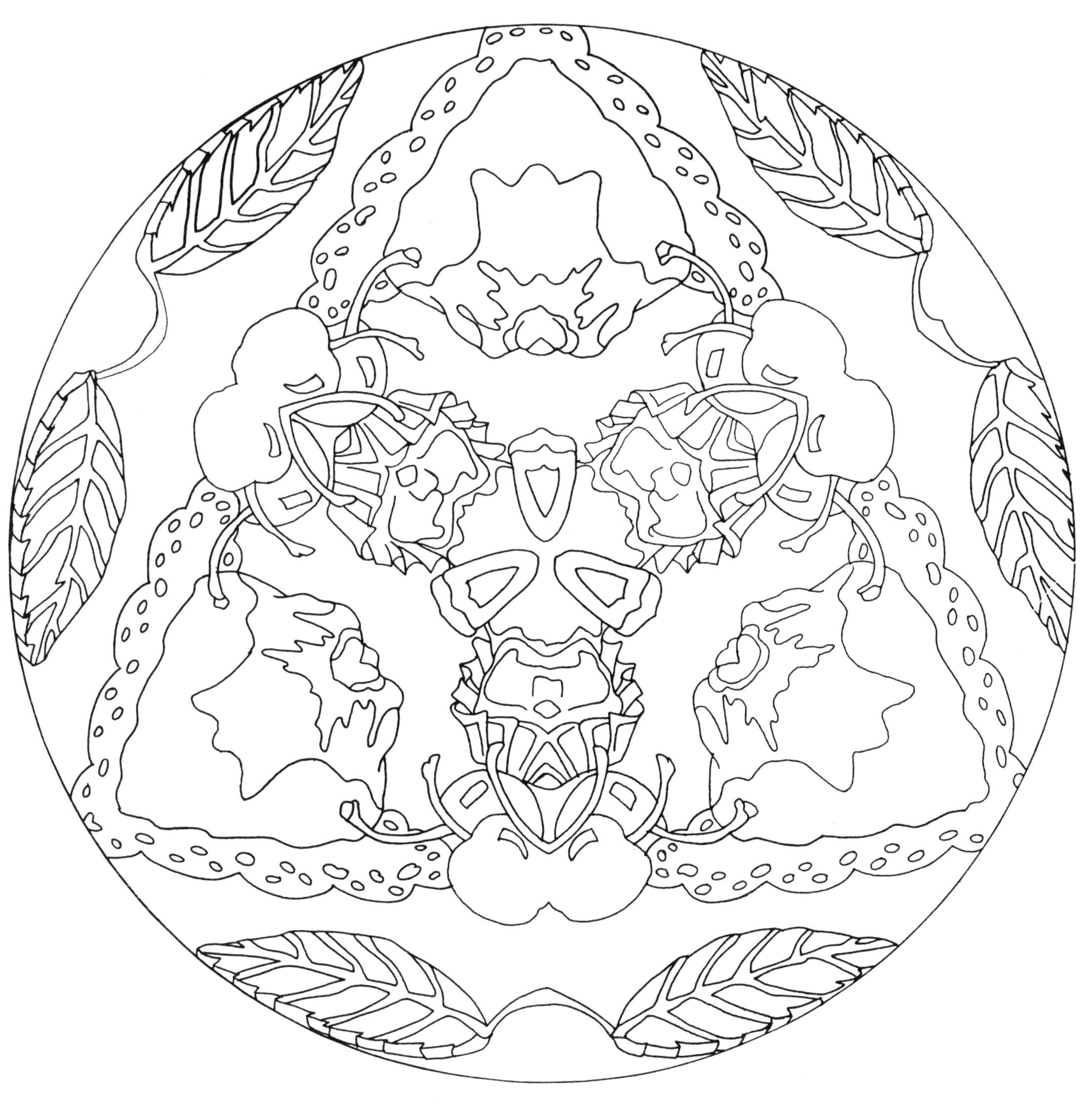

PLATE 32 "Chocolate D.G.'s."

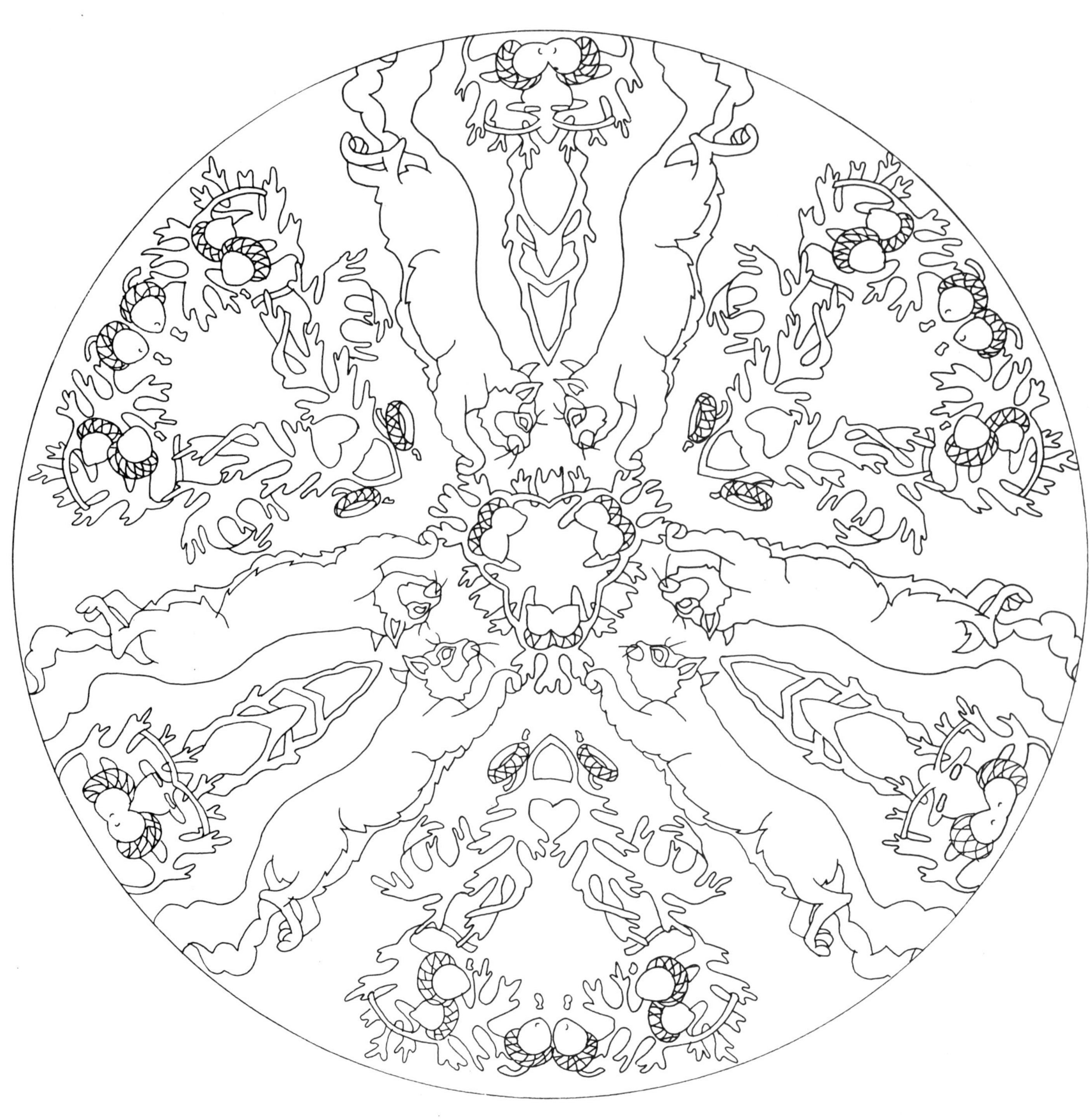

PLATE 33 "Harvest Time."

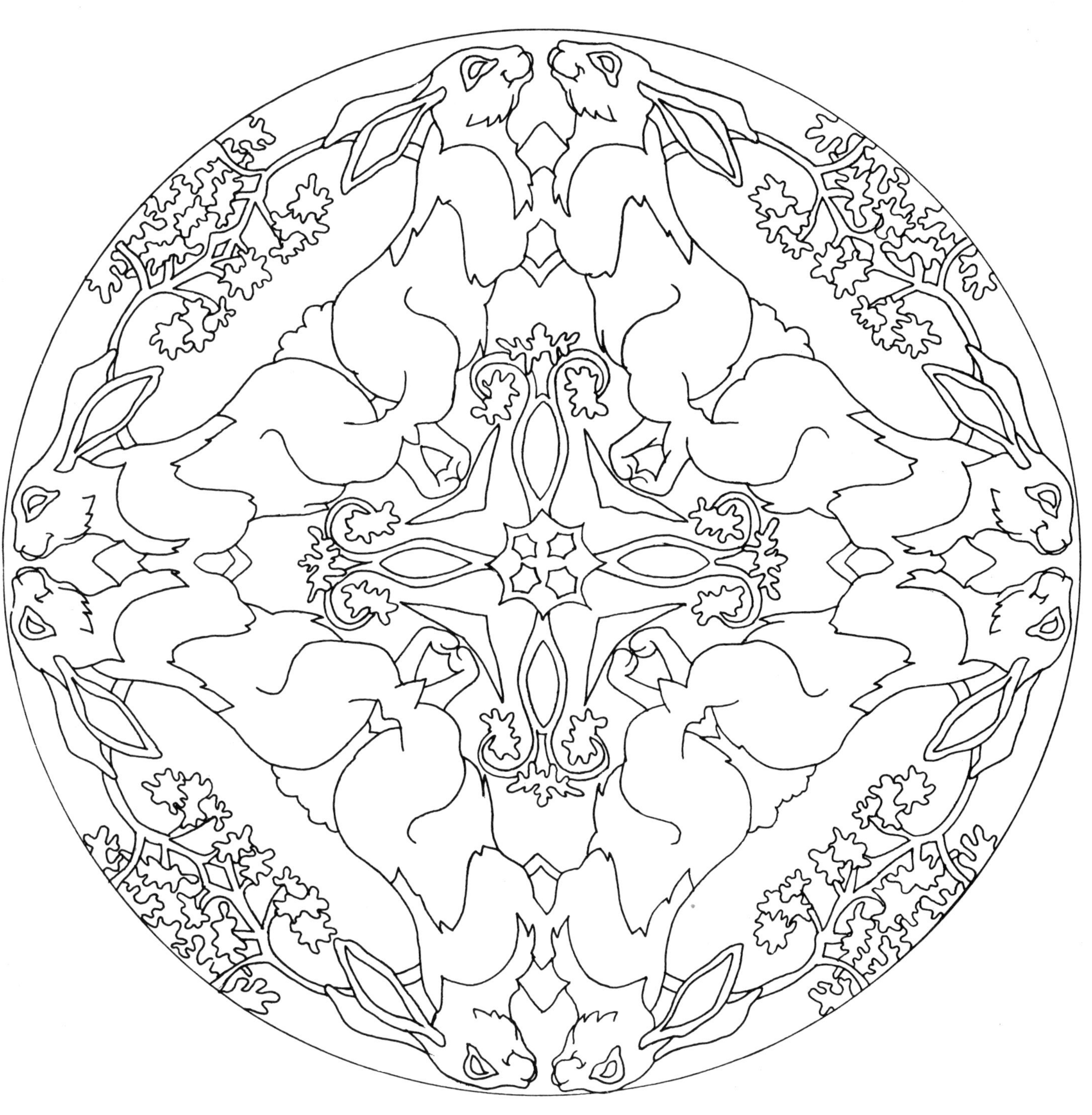

PLATE 34 "Brer and Ms."

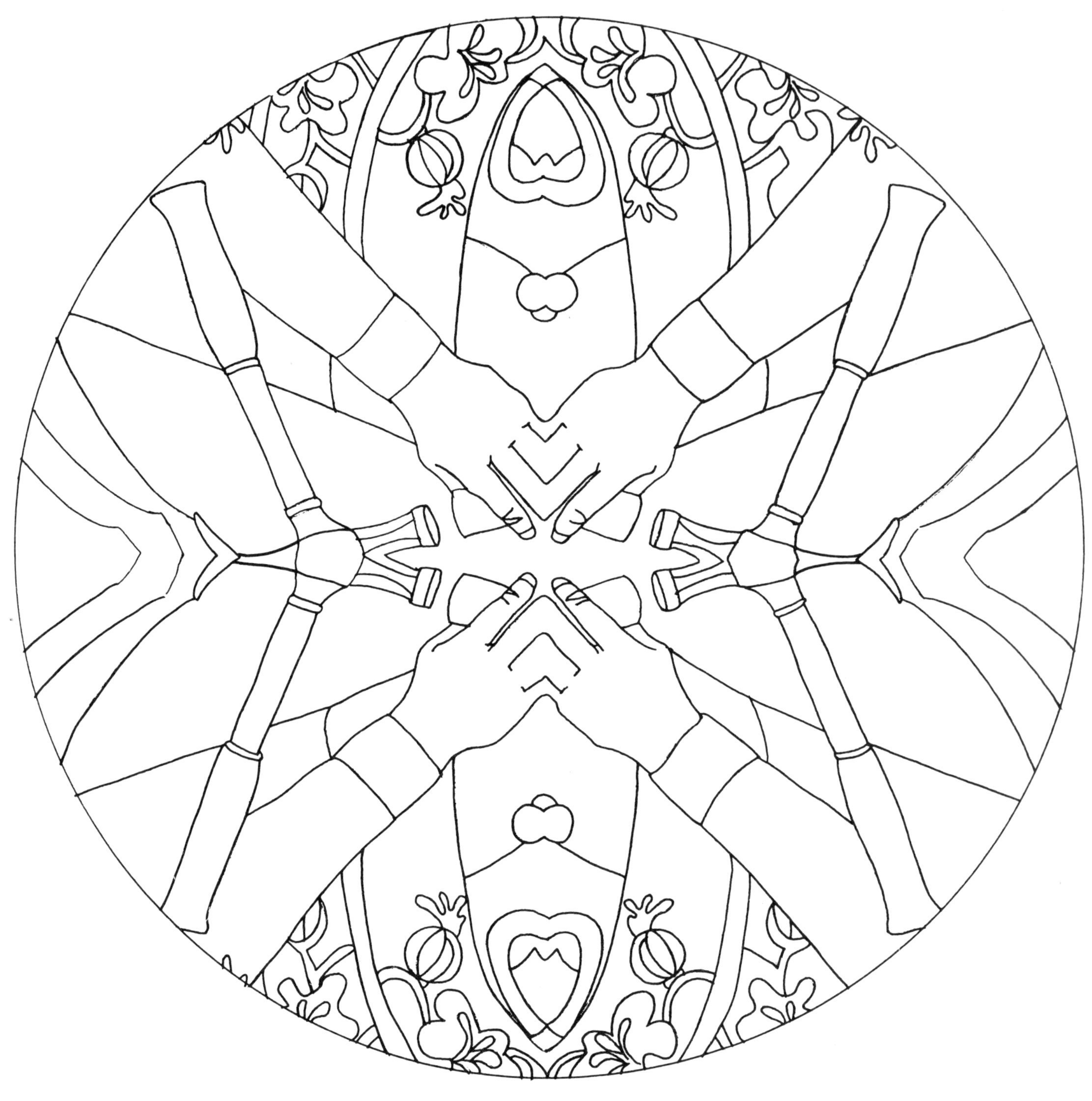

PLATE 35 "Tools of the Trade."

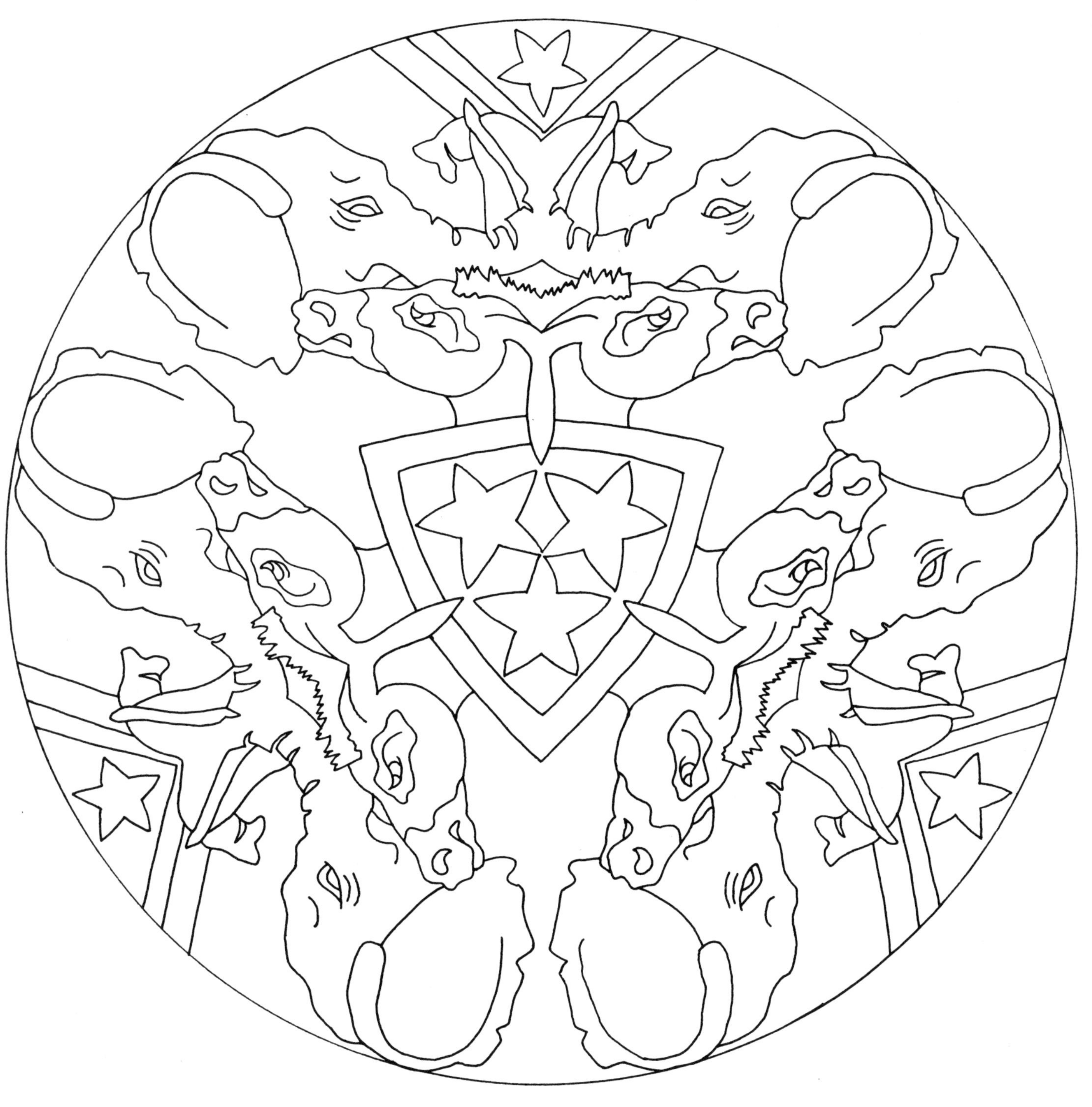

PLATE 36 "Tug-o-War, 1980."

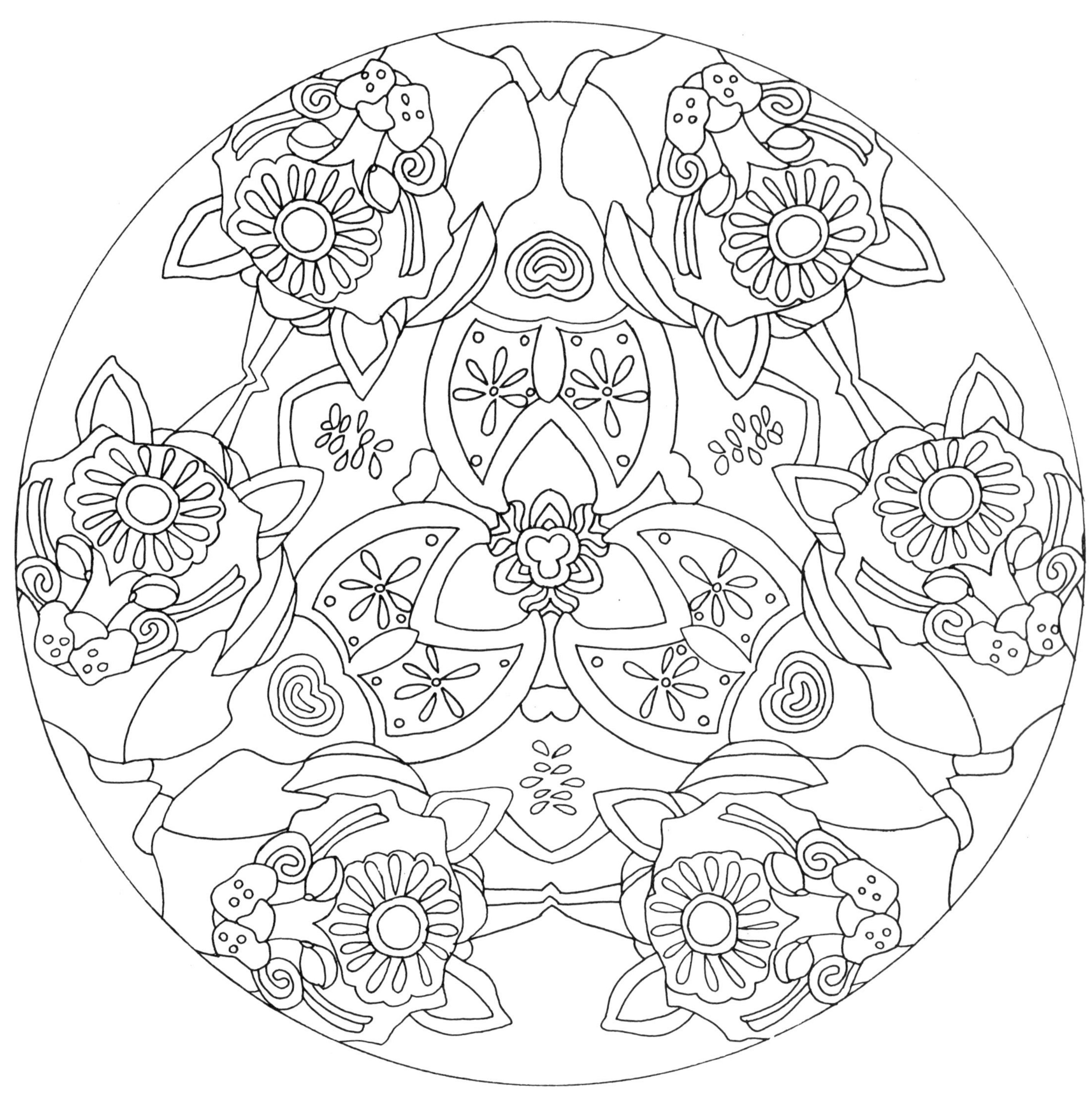

PLATE 37 "Kutani Feline."

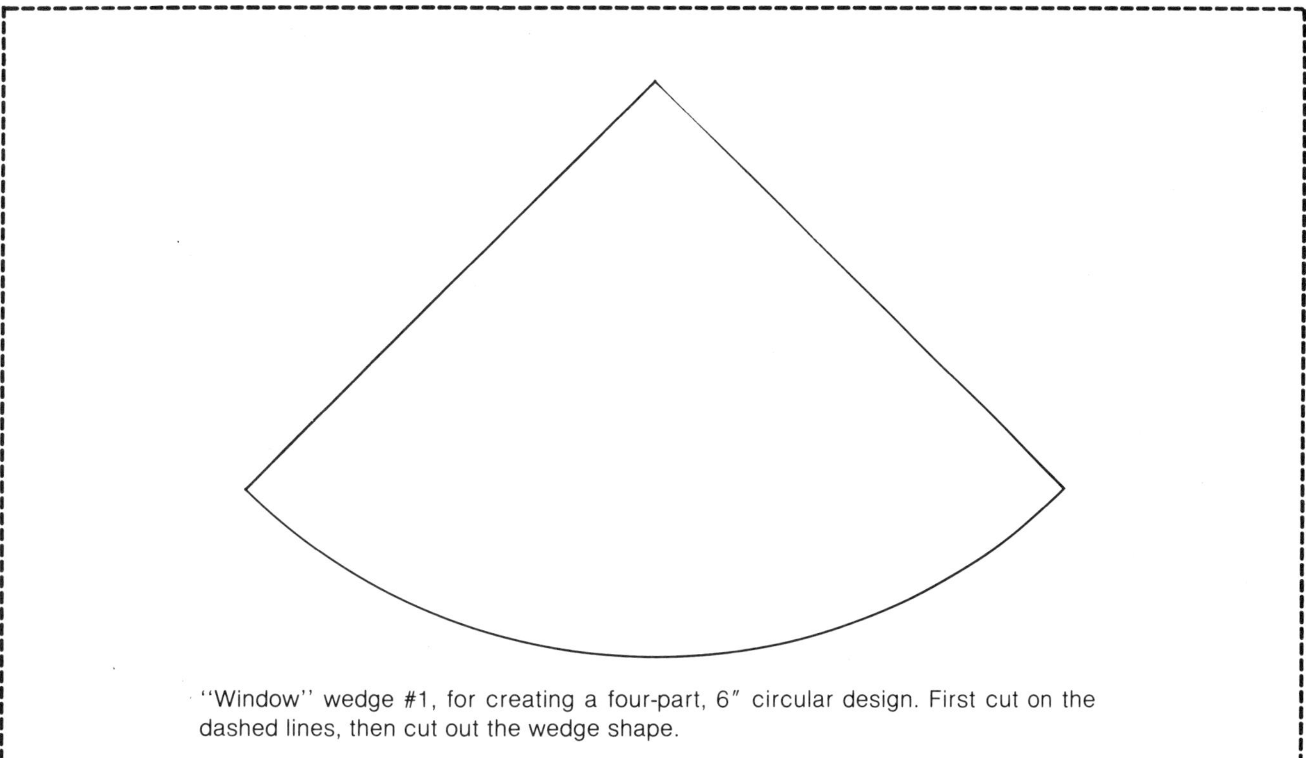

"Window" wedge #1, for creating a four-part, 6″ circular design. First cut on the dashed lines, then cut out the wedge shape.

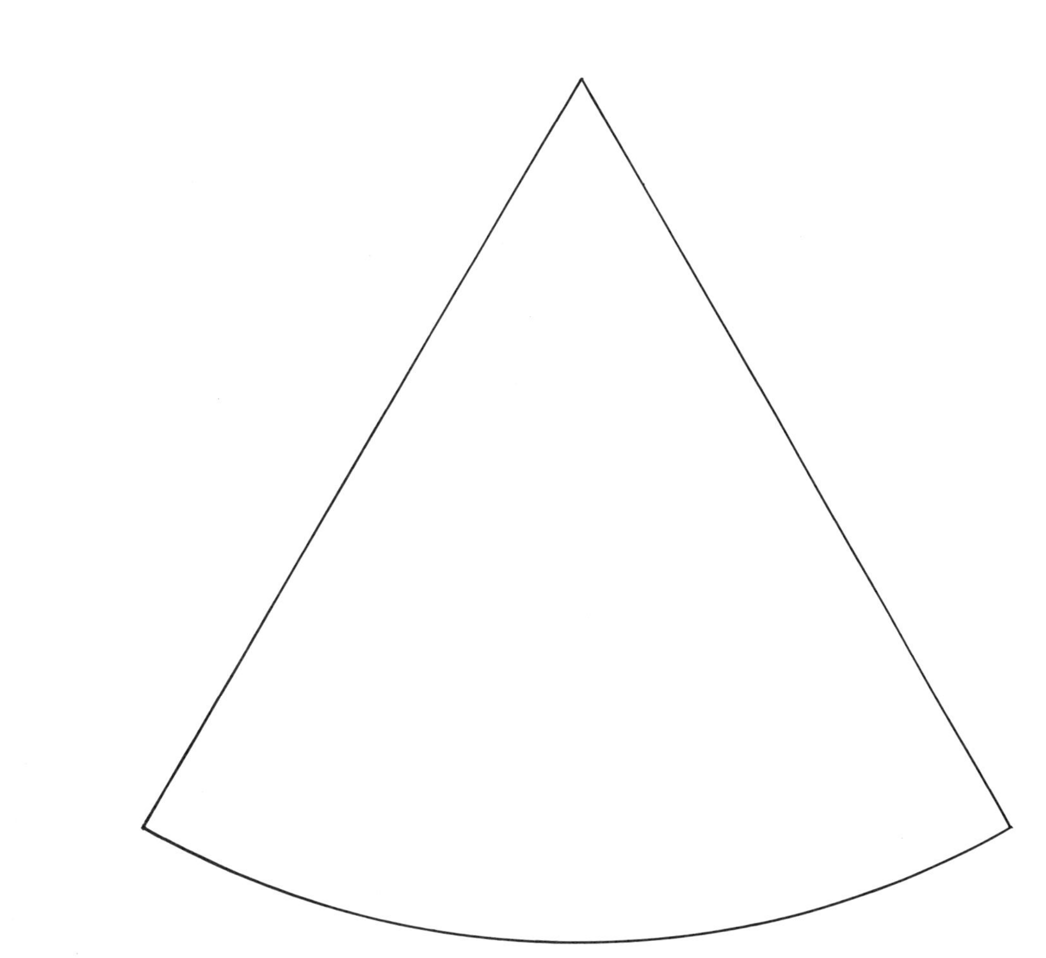

"Window" wedge #2, for creating a six-part, 9″ design. First cut on the dashed lines, then cut out the wedge shape.

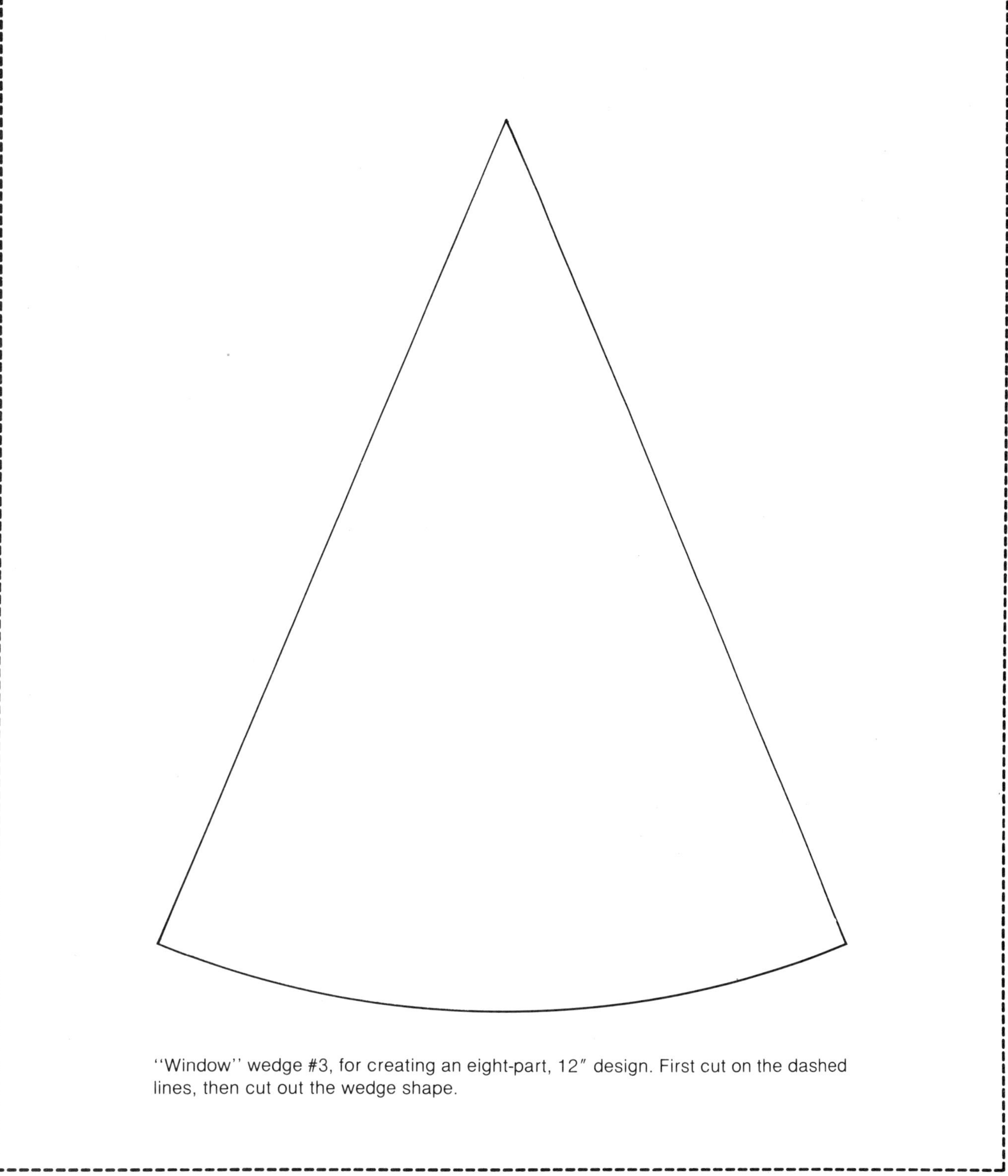

"Window" wedge #3, for creating an eight-part, 12″ design. First cut on the dashed lines, then cut out the wedge shape.